CONCILIUM

THEOLOGY IN THE AGE OF RENEWAL

CONCILIUM

CONCILIUM / VOL. 17

CHURCH HISTORY

HISTORICAL INVESTIGATIONS

Volume 17

CONCILIUM
theology in the age of renewal

PAULIST PRESS
NEW YORK, N.Y. / GLEN ROCK, N.J.

The Imprimatur for this volume applies only to articles by Roman Catholic authors.

NIHIL OBSTAT: Joseph F. Donahue, S.J., S.T.L.
Censor Deputatus

IMPRIMATUR: ✠ Bernard J. Flanagan, D.D.
Bishop of Worcester

August 19, 1966

The Nihil Obstat and Imprimatur are official declarations that a book or pamphlet is free of doctrinal or moral error. No implication is contained therein that those who have granted the Nihil Obstat and Imprimatur agree with the contents, opinions or statements expressed.

Library of Congress Catalogue Card Number: 66-29260

Suggested Decimal Classification: 270

BOOK DESIGN: Claude Ponsot

Paulist Press assumes responsibility for the accuracy of the English translations in this Volume.

PAULIST PRESS
EXECUTIVE OFFICES: 304 W. 58th Street, New York, N.Y. and 21 Harristown Road, Glen Rock, N.J.
Executive Publisher: John A. Carr, C.S.P.
Executive Manager: Alvin A. Illig, C.S.P.
Asst. Executive Manager: Thomas E. Comber, C.S.P.

EDITORIAL OFFICES: 304 W. 58th Street, New York, N.Y.
Editor: Kevin A. Lynch, C.S.P.
Managing Editor: Urban P. Intondi

Printed and bound in the United States of America by The Colonial Press Inc., Clinton, Mass.

CONTENTS

vii

PART II

BIBLIOGRAPHICAL SURVEY

PART III

DO-C DOCUMENTATION CONCILIUM

PART I
ARTICLES

Victor Conzemius/*Dublin, Ireland*

The Necessity of a Scientific Treatment of Contemporary Church History

A church historian who has published some first-class works on contemporary church history once told me that some of his colleagues looked down a little on his specialty, treating it indulgently as something not quite admissible as research in the professional sense. They thought that genuine church history came to an end, at best, with the Reformation; anything after that period was a kind of forbidden preserve, with at most a few poachers sneaking out small game, whereas an ecclesiastical historian alive to the responsibilities of his calling would keep out of modern times. His smile as he told me all this showed what little respect he had for such opinions. He did not think that his professional honor was any the less secure, and he was not the least shaken in his intention to carry on his research into modern church history.

Perhaps this is a very extreme case of a negative response to the value of modern church history. Nevertheless, in Europe at least, any specialist in the field is familiar with this kind of attitude, albeit in a less pointed form. Sometimes, of course, the beginning of the closed season for scholarly work on church history is set a little later: the French Revolution or the pontificate of Leo XIII. But until only a short while ago, there were few church historians who undertook scientifically purposeful research into the 20th century and encouraged young research workers to do likewise.

There are various reasons for this attitude. A certain snobbishness may play its part, as also, perhaps, the fear of rekindling controversies that have scarcely been laid to rest. The Catholic historian in particular must find it difficult making his way through what has been hostile territory since the 18th century. Surely, then, it must be more edifying (and consoling) to research the period in which Christianity was preparing its rise to power, or the centuries during which the medieval Church was at the peak of its ascendency. In a time that was content to substitute erudition for historical science, proposing a new thesis on the author of the *Imitatio Christi* was a means of assuring oneself an academic and ecclesiastical respectability. The author of a work on the Enlightenment, the French Revolution or the origins of radicalism had little prospect of a similar reward. If he tried for one honor, he could be certain that the other would escape him.

It is not my task here to analyze the reasons for this inadequate regard for modern church history. Of course, serious objections have been advanced against the study of modern and contemporary history. Its respectability has been questioned in secularist circles. Harvard historian H. Stuart Hughes relates how, in his undergraduate days, it was said that a subject in European history had to be one hundred years old before it was suitably mature for academic inspection; the years since the French Revolution were given the suspect label of "contemporary history".[1] Discussions of the possibility, concept and compass of contemporary history have been carried on among secularist historians for many years.[2] The two most important arguments against the

---

[1] H. St. Hughes, "History as Art and as Science," in *World Perspectives* 32 (New York, 1964), p. 89.

[2] M. Bendiscioli, *Possibilità e limiti di una storia critica degli avvenimenti comtemporanei* (Salerno, 1954); H. Rothfels, "Zeitgeschichte as Aufgabe," in *Vierteljahrshefte für Zeitgeschichte,* 1 (1953); *idem, Zeitgeschichtliche Betrachtungen* (Göttingen, 1959); B. Scheurig, *Einführung in die Zeitgeschichte* (Berlin, 1962); H. St. Hughes, *op. cit.,* pp. 89-107 ("Is Contemporary History Real History?").

study of contemporary history are inadequate distance from the events and unsatisfactory documentary evidence. I shall return to these objections later. My own position, which I intend to justify in the substance of this article, is as follows: There is such a thing as contemporary church history; it is a concern of scientific church history, and there are actual possibilities and valid conditions for its practice.

I

The Basis of a Scientific Study of Church History

The history of the Church is the history of the kingdom of God on earth. More precisely, it is the history of the People of God under way in space and time toward the heavenly Jerusalem. Faith supplies church history with its object, but the object is described and expostulated with the aid of the instruments of empirical research. The nature of the Church is itself "theandric", being a commingling of divine and human realities, and the history of the Church results from the interaction of these constituent elements. Therefore, church history is neither the history of religion nor of Christianity. It is the study of faith. It is not a purely descriptive secular science, for it derives its standards of value from both faith and scientific scholarship.[3]

The question then arises: Does faith itself offer an objection to the study of contemporary church history? And there is an answer: "The Church," says the *Dogmatic Constitution on the Church:* " '. . . presses forward amid the persecutions of the world and the consolations of God', announcing the cross and death of the Lord until he comes (cf. 1 Cor. 11, 26). By the power of the risen Lord it is given strength that it might, in patience and in love, overcome its sorrows and its challenges, both within itself and from without, and that it might reveal to the world, even though dimly, yet faithfully, the mystery of its Lord

[3] Cf. on this point the introductions by R. Aubert and H. Jedin to their church histories.

until, finally, it will be manifested in full light." [4] This would exclude certain interpretations of church history, and particularly the "decline theory", which regards the era of the early Church as a "golden age" after which the course of church history has gone into gradual decline. The "progress theory", which stems from the Enlightenment and according to which the Church gradually attains perfection as the centuries pass, becomes likewise untenable. Both these conceptions are contradicted by the teaching of the Church.

For the same reason, it would not be permissible to argue the primary importance of contemporary church history on pragmatic grounds. However, this does not necessarily mean that the history of the Church is a linear progression. The growth of the Church is not a uniform process; it does not move through the centuries with the smoothness of a sturdy ship sailing a calm sea. There are storms; the tides of world history rise and fall, sometimes violently. Nor does the Church journey to its supernatural destination in a fully automated trailer; it is constantly adapting itself to the various conditions along the route. And it is certainly quite permissible for the historian to pay more adequate attention to periods of crisis and upheaval in the history of the Church. For the purposes of such an analysis, it is enough to know that the Church draws strength at all times from the life of the resurrected Christ, and that it always retains the promise of the Holy Spirit. It is erroneous to maintain that the Holy Spirit inspired only the primitive and medieval Church, and that his influence is scarcely apparent in modern times. Through faith, one can see the loyalty of God as the most constant element in the history of the Church. God did not abandon the Church of our own times, and the church historian also benefits from his promise: "I am with you always, to the close of the age."

[4] *Constitution on the Church* (Glen Rock, N.J.: Paulist Press, 1965), p. 75.

II

CONTEMPORARY CHURCH HISTORY AS A CONCERN OF SCIENTIFIC CHURCH HISTORY

Faith, therefore, does not present any obstacle to the study of the contemporary history of the Church. Even the most recent phase of the past life of the Church is history influenced by the Holy Spirit, to no lesser degree than any other period more distant in time. However, I still have to show whether the human component of church history—the methodology and science of history—can legitimately admit the study of contemporary church history. Since the historian has direct access only to the human aspect of the Church, and since I am concerned in my inquiry with the problem of the historical methodology, I shall concentrate my argument on this point.

First of all, a few words are necessary on the limits of contemporary church history. Without contesting the accepted periodization, contemporary church history is understood here as the period inaugurated by the French Revolution, or, to express it in another way, the Church in the industrial age. Contemporary church history in the more recent sense would begin with World War I—the decisive turning point of modern times.

Secular historians sometimes set the beginning of contemporary history at the fall of Bismarck (1890),[5] but the fall of the German chancellor does not have the same significance for the history of the Church. Even the measurement of historical time according to the reigns of different popes no longer seems meaningful. But the upheaval brought about by World War I is of worldwide historical significance. There is no further profit to be gained from examining the question of periodization: it is enough to confirm that the research into modern church history since the French Revolution and, more especially, the period since the death of Pius IX, has been inadequate. Only a few isolated historical accounts treat of this later period.

[5] G. Barraclough, *An Introduction to Contemporary History* (London, 1964), p. 2.

The question whether there is such a thing as contemporary church history presupposes yet another problem: Is research into contemporary history itself possible? Whatever the particular problems of contemporary historical studies may be, one cannot deny the remarkable fact that the most signicant works of Western history were written as contemporary history. Herodotus, Thucydides, Tacitus, Froissart, Commines and Guicciardini were all contemporary historians.[6] For the historian, the most valuable passages in the writings of the early church historians—from Eusebius and his successors down through the annalists, chroniclers and historiographers of the Middle Ages—are those dealing with the times the authors knew through personal experience. This means that contemporary history is not simply something that came into vogue after 1928, as if in answer to a disillusioned public anxiously demanding why "the war to end all wars" had not quite worked out like that.[7]

It is even more pertinent to ask whether the present bias against the study of contemporary history is not a descendant of that 19th-century academicism which—blinded by assumptions peculiar to the time—called into question its claim to scientific validity. Not very long ago "scientific" historical research itself had to plead for full academic recognition. The opinion that the function of the science of history should be an entirely objective research into the past for its own sake is thoroughly outdated; not so, however, the idea that the examination of contemporary events is a valid task for the historian.[8]

Benedetto Croce reacted sharply against the confident academicism of the 19th century when he stated that all history was contemporary history: "The practical requirements that underlie every historical judgment give to all history the character of 'contemporary history', because, however remote in time events thus recounted may seem to be, the history in reality refers to present

[6] H. Seton-Watson, "A Plea for the Study of Contemporary History," in *History* 14 (1929), p. 4.

[7] G. Barraclough, *op. cit.*, p. 7.

[8] F. Ernst, "Zeitgeschehen und Geschichtsschreibung," in *Die Welt als Geschichte* 17 (1957), pp. 137-89.

needs and present situations wherein those events vibrate." [9]
Clearly, the main task of the historian is not to record, but to
evaluate with understanding, ". . . for, if he does not evaluate,
how can he know what is worth recording?" [10]

III

Is Contemporary History Possible?

The fact that such a thing as the study of contemporary history actually does exist is more conclusive than the theoretical
discussion of its possibility. There is no need to demonstrate that
contemporary history is truly scientific study; it has long since
proved its claim to legitimacy and is now an indispensable part of
modern historical research. Interest in contemporary history has
been given a firm impetus by two world wars. As world-shattering
catastrophes they forced research workers to examine their multi-
farious causes.

The tradition of American historical studies has enjoyed a
more pragmatic orientation, and American historians have found
the approach to contemporary history less difficult. In Europe,
as well, the study of contemporary history has come to stay as
a serious and scientifically responsible department of historical
research. France has its *Commission d'histoire de la Résistance*
and a *Comité d'histoire de la deuxième guerre mondiale* with
its own archives and journal.[11] In Munich there is an institute for
contemporary history which has published a scholarly quarterly
since 1953. The English medievalist Geoffrey Barraclough sees
nothing objectionable in our writing a contemporary work on
20th-century world history.

Contemporary historical studies have been particularly strong
in postwar Germany, where a large number of books and articles
dealing with questions of the recent past have appeared since

[9] B. Croce, *History as the Story of Liberty* (Eng. tr.: London, 1941),
p. 19; quoted by E. L. Carr, *op. cit. infra*, p. 15.
[10] E. L. Carr, *What Is History?* (London, 1961), p. 15.
[11] H. Michel, *Revue Historique* 89 (1965), pp. 127-38.

1945. There is also some reason to think that contemporary history has played a more substantial part than formerly in the syllabus for upper forms of German secondary schools. The anguished question, "How could things have gone so far?", has naturally been a powerful spur to keeping this interest alive. German history of the last few centuries suddenly appeared in another light. Apart from some beneficial judgments, this critical questioning of the accepted picture of German history has also led to hasty revisions and unhistorical simplifications. Some historians thought that they were now duty-bound to scour German history for possible forerunners of National Socialism—perhaps considering themselves an extension of the commission for tracing Nazi war criminals. But these extravagances do not invalidate the study of contemporary history. In those areas where the traditional methodology of historical research has been used to investigate precise and timely problems for which authentic sources were available, considerable results have already been obtained. In this connection we could cite such examples as the Weimar Republic, the development of the major political parties and detailed questions relating to military history.

The assumption of power by totalitarian nazism exposed the Christian Churches in Germany to major upheavals. The Evangelical Church suffered most under this trial. After the appointment of a *Reichsbischof,* the "Confessional Church" seceded from the National Church and the regional establishments. It was not long before this body became involved in a bitter ecclesiastical struggle—the *Kirchenkampf.* Since these disputes touched on questions concerning the constitution and structure of the regional Churches, postwar German Protestantism was acutely interested in the history of the conflict.

As early as 1955, in conjunction with the University of Hamburg, the "Commission To Examine the History of the Church-Conflict in the Nazi Period" was established. To date, it has been able to publish approximately fifteen major research papers, including an extensive bibliography on the *Kirchenkampf.* At a relatively late date, the Roman Catholic side realized the need for a scientific treatment of National Socialist church politics. It was presumed that a few occasional contributions and publications of the postwar period would satisfy an historically aware public in search of information. To this can be traced the origin of the belief that the Catholic Church in Germany consciously cultivated a "resistance myth"—an idea that the hard facts do not justify.

The controversies that have been carried on, somewhat acrimoniously, since 1960 have accelerated isolated attempts to ensure that research into this complex of issues is undertaken on a scientific basis. In 1963, the Commission for the Study of Contemporary History was established at the *Katholische Akademie* in Bavaria; its first publication appeared after 1965. It was a sensible decision not to restrict the commission to the study of the *Kirchenkampf,* but, rather, to include the development of the Christian political parties and concordat politics.[12]

Somewhat earlier, a research institute for contemporary church history was founded in Austria. In 1961, the Institute for Contemporary Church History was established in Salzburg within the framework of the International Research Center for basic questions affecting the sciences. Apart from the total complex of the "Roman Question" and the concordats of modern times, this institute is concerned—with special reference to German-speaking Europe—with an examination of the following areas: the *Kulturkampf,* or Church-State conflict, in both the 19th and 20th centuries; the position of the Church with respect to the various nationalities of the former Austro-Hungarian Empire; the relations between the Church and National Socialism; the history of the Christian social movement; the development of the Christian concept of toleration, and the attitude of the Church to the world from Vatican Council I to Vatican Council II.[13]

[12] Cf. J. Nobecourt, "Les catholiques allemands en face de leur passé," in *Etudes* (June, 1965), pp. 789-808.

[13] I am indebted to Prof. Dr. Erika Weinzierl-Fischer, Director of the Institute, for this information.

IV

A Scientific Study of Contemporary
Church History Is a Necessity

In German-speaking Europe, the suasions to deal more thoroughly with the most recent period of church history have been for the most part external. However, the Churches of other countries have also been shaken in their self-assurance of possessing national, spiritual and cultural assets. The end of European imperialism, the collapse of colonialism, the technologization of the world, the successful progress of communism and the de-Europeanization of our conception of history do not serve merely to emphasize the pressing need for a pastoral *aggiornamento*.

Church history, too, is "vibrating" [Croce's phrase] within the context of the contemporary life of the Church. The Church of today is inquiring into its past. This has not provoked any revolution in doctrine, for the continuity of the Church's proclamation has not been called in question. But it has opened up the Church to its own past and to today's world. The light shed by the Council on the history of the Church has affected research into church history and has managed to illuminate the past, altering some of our former conceptions in the process. Perhaps the most striking is the reevaluation of the Council of Constance, marked among Catholic scholars for the last few years.[14]

One still hopes that a ray of light will shine from the Council of our own age into the darkness where Catholic reform movements and such intellectual manifestations as Episcopalism, Josephinism and the Enlightenment still languish as victims of the Church's official chroniclers. Individuals and movements that have been treated only marginally by church historians are the object of rediscovery. Europe's feeling of superiority has received some healthy knocks. One can no longer lump together the history of the Church in the British Commonwealth, in South America and in the mission countries as tiresome and uninteresting

[14] A. Franzen, "The Council of Constance: Present State of the Problem," in *Concilium* 7: *Historical Problems of Church Renewal* (Glen Rock, N.J.: Paulist Press, 1965), pp. 29-68.

appendages of the history of the Church in Europe. It must set a church historian thinking when he learns that there is still no history of the Church in South America.[15]

A more impartial evaluation of the Reformation was initiated in Roman Catholic circles long before the Council, but there is still much meticulous historical work to be done before the "gold-content of the fragments separated from the gold-bearing stratum" has been exactly assayed (to retain Pius XI's metaphor for the separated Christian Churches). Of course, this will also entail the possibility of superficial reconciliations, historical *non-sequiturs,* deceptive simplifications and premature canonizations, but the historian must take this risk, just as he must expect that his conscientious and laborious research will be reduced to a footnote in the reference works of tomorrow.

The Council has given church history a new impetus. But the necessity for a scientific study of contemporary church history, in particular, deserves special insistence if the Church is to see and understand itself more exactly. Two examples will serve to make this clearer.

Catholic research into Vatican Council I only began, in any real sense, with the announcement of Vatican Council II. The official documents appeared relatively late—more than fifty years after the closing of the Council—and the editorial work can hardly be considered first class. In the meantime, historians inimical to the Council had enough leisure to present the weaknesses of conciliar decisions in a prejudicial light. Such Roman Catholic historians as Thomas Granderath, S.J., who had to undertake the unenviable role of "official" historiographers, were now forced to take up a defensive position. They had to contradict and seek to rectify. It is hardly surprising that they were not always successful. Protestant historians of Vatican Council I up to Mc-Gregor and Harding Meyer[16] placed more confidence in a rebel-

[15] E. Dussel, "Vers une histoire de l'Eglise d'Amérique latine," in *Esprit* (June/August, 1965).

[16] G. McGregor, *The Vatican Revolution* (London, 1958); H. Meyer, "Das Wort Pius IX: Die Tradition bin ich," in *Theologische Existenz heute* 122 (Munich, 1965).

lious Catholic than in an "official" historian, and for quite intelligible reasons. This is yet another confirmation of that conspicuous lack of a sense of public relations for which, as R. Aubert has remarked in another context, ecclesiastical authorities, and the Vatican in particular, have been justly reproached.[17]

Anyone who looked on Protestants and non-Christians as "underlings of the devil" could remain happily indifferent to their opinions about Vatican Council I. But the Catholic theologian who today follows the intention of the *Decree on Ecumenism,* and who attempts an objective appreciation of the teaching on infallibility, continually encounters gross misconceptions for which the late awakening of Catholic church historians in writing on Vatican Council I is partly responsible.

In yet another sense, this delay has worked to the advantage of the Church's understanding of itself in its effect on Vatican Council II. Until a short while ago, only inexact and sketchy introductions to the work, projects and intellectual trends at Vatican Council I and to the evolution and content of its conciliar decrees were available. A thorough revision of unsolved problems of Vatican Council I would have given the preparatory conciliar commissions and the Council fathers an advantageous start and a better basis of discussion, at least for some important theological points. In the light of Vatican Council I, which is naturally as relevant for all the fathers as the Council of our own times, Vatican Council II appears less revolutionary than anyone unacquainted with recent church history would think.

Other indications that the Catholic church historian should no longer be idle even in the field of most recent contemporary history have been given by the debates, especially pronounced in Germany, on the Church and nazism, on the papacy and the murder of the Jews, and on Christianity and the "Jewish Question". The modern world does not have the patience to wait until questions of the immediate past are declared "mature" enough

---

[17] R. Aubert, "Religious Liberty from 'Mirari Vos' to the 'Syllabus,'" in *Concilium 7: Historical Problems of Church Renewal* (Glen Rock, N.J.: Paulist Press, 1965), pp. 89-105.

for historical study. Furthermore, who is to make such a declaration? It wants an answer now, in our own times, from immediately available sources. If the professional historian refuses to give an answer, then the amateur will step forward, only too happy to present his piquant opinions to the public in the language of "common sense", unburdened by historical reflection. Shakespeare, Racine and Schiller were more modest when they used historical material; they did not masquerade as professional historians. The opportunity was open for the German dramatist Rolf Hochhuth, in his play *The Deputy,* not only to tackle a genuine problem, but also to "deputize" himself as a contemporary ecclesiastical historian. The dramatic value of his play is a matter of opinion, but there can be no doubt, at least for the historian, concerning the quality of its documentary appendices. With obdurate incredulity, Hochhuth has insisted that his selective and prepared documentation has value as historical evidence, but if any aspect of his work is incompetent, this is it. Professional historians were, to some extent, unable to offer any criticism, since they had no access to pertinent sources. In the meantime, Hochhuth's example and method have been imitated by a number of others; he has also received covering fire from professional historians: for example, G. Lewy and S. Friedländer.[18] These writers approach their subject with selective partiality or with an uncritical faith in certain sources. The unhistorical nature of their standards is usually revealed in the concluding section of their works.

For wide areas of public opinion throughout the world, the play about Pope Pius XII and the murder of the Jews and the historical works that have appeared in its wake confirm a certain picture of the relationship between the Church and nazism. Even among Catholics certain false conceptions and legends about the modern papacy have gained a measure of currency.

The historian again finds himself in the unpleasant position of

[18] G. Lewy, *The Catholic Church and Nazi Germany* (New York, 1964); S. Friedländer, *Pie XII et le IIIe Reich—Documents* (Paris, 1964). The writer of the present article is preparing a bibliography of the literature on the *Kirchenkampf* for the *Revue d'histoire ecclésiastique.*

having to rectify and correct; this task—not particularly attractive in itself—will not be made any easier for him if he writes as an "official" historiographer. *The Deputy* and its heirs are therefore typical of circumstances in which contemporary church history has failed its responsibility. The questions were somehow definitely in the air and informed contemporary church historians had an opportunity to anticipate critical comment. One can only deplore the fact that studies of the problems of contemporary church history connected with nazism and fascism were not co-ordinated by an international commission in which competent non-Catholics would necessarily have been included.

V

POSSIBILITIES AND PRE-CONDITIONS

But, the reader might say, does this not all go to prove that the nearer one is to the events under observation, the more impossible impartial and objective contemporary studies become? There are a considerable number of biographies of important figures of the 19th century as well as a few individual works on the church history of the 19th century, on recent papal history and on the *Kulturkampf* that were written a few years after the events or pontificates in question but which have now been "superseded". Does this not underscore the impossibility of a study of contemporary church history?

To this I would answer that until now our study of contemporary church history has been something between more or less dignified journalism and a form of panegyric more closely akin to apologetics. The borderline is hazy; in most cases, it is a mixture of the two. To this same category belong the rancorous exposés written in reaction to this adulatory literature. But even these latter are not the more valuable because they go to the opposite extreme.

Multi-volume biographies with long extracts from correspondence, linked to one another with a few generalized remarks, and pesudo-hagiographical lives of popes are not contemporary history.[19] Nor can true history be rendered superfluous by ecclesiastical statistics or annals. Contemporary church historians treat their themes with the methods of traditional historical writing; they must use basic sources which are exhaustive in scope. The opening-up of sources and a critical evaluation of documents are the main prerequisites for responsible research into contemporary history. However, there are other important prerequisites for all historical writing: distance and a concern for objectivity. Professional distance from the subject under discussion is extremely important if history is not to degenerate into biased axe-grinding.

In spite of the greater distance in time, a convinced anti-curialist, an extreme papalist or a dogmatic Marxist will bring his preconceptions into the study of medieval history. The medievalist also must achieve that inner distance from his theme that the contemporary historian, perhaps, has to strive after even more meticulously on account of his personal or existential interest in the events. Up to now we have not found any insurmountable obstacle in the way of the writing of contemporary history. The most serious objections that can now be raised against it are untrustworthy sources and inadequate documentation.

To these objections one is inclined to answer that contemporary history is in a privileged position, since many of its sources have been made available through the press and publicity. This does not apply, however, to the sources of modern church history. The main source of information on the Church is not the press or publicity, or even the custodian of the Vatican archives, but God himself. This is the most important source of all, yet it remains closed to the church historian throughout his lifetime. As befits its nature as an institution of religious mediation, the Church is cautious in its "publicity releases". But it is precisely this congenital dearth of exact information that should prompt responsible authorities to make accessible, after a reasonable pe-

[19] Offensive books like those by Nazareno Padellaro and Konstantin, Prince of Bavaria, are partly responsible for originating a displeasing mythology about Pius XII; these books have earned mention in the index of sins against good taste.

riod of time, those documents in ecclesiastical archives that relate to an important phase in the Church's development. But it is impossible to lay down a hard and fast principle, since a sudden insurgence of historical interest can make a determined period of reticence absurd.

There is no doubt that the present Vatican restrictions concerning the unavailability of material subsequent to 1846 do not correspond to contemporary historical requirements. A suitable change is therefore urgently required, not merely to satisfy the curiosity of historians, but in order to give interested sections of the public a satisfactory picture of the Church. The biased publication of existing documents in national or private archives has produced a truly "one-sided" picture of developments in the Church. Historical perspectives have been falsified, and considerable damage has occasionally been done. The excessive delay of ecclesiastical circles in the publication of documents is to some degree responsible for the production of new "papal legends".[20] Therefore, one has every reason to be grateful that the moratorium of fifty years observed hitherto has been broken with the publication of the documentary series *La Saint-Siège et la guerre en Europe*.[21] Until now, the usual answer was something like this: "One must not inquire too closely into the affairs of those who are still alive." However, the Church is alive; it, and not the office-holders and functionaries, is the bestower of life. Statesmen and politicians of our own times have to suffer sharp criticisms from contemporary historians, and the most experienced ecclesiastical functionary has the human right to factual error. If once faulted for an incorrect appreciation of a certain situation, no one's human dignity is dishonored (and especially not that of clerics vowed to humility and fully conscious of their condition as human beings). The "public image" of the Church is more important than that of ecclesiastical officials.

When Pope John XXIII's *Journal of a Soul* appeared a few years ago, some people remarked that it was not a wise decision

---

[20] B. Schneider, "Moderne Papstfabeln," in *Archivum Historiae Pontificiae* 2 (1964), pp. 329-38.

[21] Rome, 1965.

to disclose, in so unvarnished and naïve a way, the Italian seminary education of a certain period and what seems to us nowadays the somewhat unusual asceticism of Pope John's period of training. Anyone expressing so stuffy an opinion revealed his complete lack of historical perspective. *Journal of a Soul* served to cut short once and forever the beginnings of a Johannine mythology; this alone was justification enough for its early publication. But it also revealed a magnificent expression of the action of God's grace in this man, which took him out of the smallness and narrowness of his spiritual beginnings into the service of the universal Church. God's compassionate understanding is greater than man can ever foresee.

Unfortunately there are too few people in the Church who have the courage of an Angelo Roncalli—too few who entrust themselves to the guidance of God. Perhaps that is the reason why the autobiographical reminiscences of some prominent ecclesiasts—the number of which is not excessive—are so astonishingly trivial! In such works they merely display their banality and narrowmindedness. Of course, the publication of such memoranda should be discouraged.

A man who undertakes his ecclesiastical responsibilities in the light of faith has no need to fear the judgments of posterity. The church historian, too, should not avoid problems of contemporary church history. He remains bound to the historian's ethic, which Leo XIII—using the impressive formulation of Cicero—has offered as a guiding motto for Catholic historical research: *Ne quid falsi dicere audeat; ne quid veri non audeat* (Let no one dare to speak falsely; let no one dare not to speak the truth).

That is no charter to write ecclesiastical party history or to drag trivial personal intrigues into the field of historical writing. John XXIII was a man who did not hesitate to write contemporary history,[22] for he put his trust in the one who sustained him in faith. One of the sayings he has left behind as part of his legacy should encourage the contemporary church historian in his task: "He who has faith does not waver."

[22] G. Roncalli wrote the biography of his bishop: *Mons. Giacomo Maria Radini Tedeschi:* I, II (1919); III (1963).

Giuseppe d'Ercole/ *Rome, Italy*

The Presbyteral Colleges in the Early Church

An article about presbyteral colleges in the early Church, written primarily according to the pastoral criteria of *Concilium,* is necessarily limited. Accordingly, one must presuppose as already discussed and resolved some problems that are preliminary to the question.[1]

I

THE APOSTOLIC ERA

(a) *The Presbyters of Jerusalem*

The first presbyteral college recorded in the New Testament is that of Jerusalem. The sources tell us nothing about the circumstances and the reasons that gave birth to the presbyters of Jeru-

---

[1] A. Michiels, *L'origine de l'Episcopat* (Paris, 1900); E. Ruffini, *La Gerarchia della Chiesa negli Atti degli Apostoli e nelle lettere di Paolo* (Rome, 1921); F. Prat, "Les dignitaires ecclésiastiques," in *La théologie de Saint Paul,* I (Paris, 1920), pp. 407ff.; G. Dix, "The Ministry in the Early Church, ca. A.D. 90-410," in *The Apostolic Ministry* (London, 1946); J. Colson, *Les fonctions ecclésiales aux premiers siècles* (Paris, 1956); M. Guerra y Gomez, *Episcopos y presbyteros. Evolución semantica de los terminos* πρεσβμτερος επισκοπος *desde Homero hasta el siglo segundo despuès de Jesu Cristo* (Burgos, 1962); P. Benoit, "Les origines apostoliques de l'Episcopat selon le Nouveau Testament," in *L'évêque dans l'église du Christ* (Bruges, 1963); G. D'Ercole, *Iter storico della formulazione delle horme costituzionali e della dottrina sui vescovi, presbiteri, laici nella Chiesa delle origini* (Rome, 1963); J. Lopez-Ortis and J. Blazquez (eds.), *El colegio episcopal* (Madrid, 1964).

salem. While the Acts narrate the circumstances of the institution
of the seven deacons, they are silent about the origin of the presbyters. They are already on the scene in the Jerusalem community when the Church of Antioch sends them the money destined
for victims of the famine then raging in Judea.[2] If we wanted to
ascertain what duties these presbyters performed, we could say
that they were the trustees and administrators of the Jerusalem
community. On the other hand, the presbyters exercise a different function in the Council of Jerusalem where they appear in the
guise of judges. Together with the apostles they resolve the controversy about the obligation of the Law and of circumcision.
While the word may seem extravagant, they are in substance leg-
islators alongside the apostles with whom they issue the doctrinal
and disciplinary decree decided by the Council.[3] Similarly, together with James they intervene in a doctrinal and disciplinary
dispute between Paul and the Judaizers. They are the conciliators,
virtually mediators, between Paul and those whose Judaic vacil-
lation leads them to criticize Saul's missionary activity.[4]

This body of presbyters exists and works in highly Judaic sur-
roundings. We cannot say when they arose because there is no
data. For the same reason we cannot explicitly establish the intention of those who appointed them. Did these presbyters perhaps arise in imitation of the Judaic institution?

I have already shown elsewhere[5] that in the Christian community of Jerusalem there grew progressively a consciousness of
being a new people distinct from the old. This consciousness arose
in the community during persecutions by the authorities of their
own nation, when many Jews rejected the new preaching. At that
time there was talk of a new people, constituted by God in his
name. Israel meanwhile came to be numbered among the Gen-
tiles.[6] Consequently, there was opposition between, and separation of, the old and the new institution. The institution of pres-

---

[2] Acts 11, 30.

[3] Acts 15, 2. 4. 6. 22. 24; 16, 4.

[4] Acts 21, 18.

[5] Cf. G. D'Ercole, *Communio, collegialità, primato e sollicitudo omnium
ecclesiarum dai Vangeli a Costantino* (Rome, 1964), pp. 83-4.

[6] Acts 2, 12; 4, 27; 15, 14.

byters completed the leadership structure of the new community, in imitation of the analogous institution of the old Israel.[7]

We might ask why this name was chosen? In reflecting on these matters, I have often observed that one fact is clear in reading the Acts and the indications of other books in the New Testament: the terms used to designate the leaders of the new institution do not repeat any of the essential terms of the Judaic structure, with the exception of presbyters. The new leaders are not called priests, and Peter, the first among them, is never designated with the term "high priest". In the new community the name of the highest ranking leaders is the twelve, the apostles. In all probability the twelve and the community believed that the unavoidable trans-formations connected with the work of Jesus and its effects would come about in a hidden way in the life of the community itself. For the time being they did not consider adopting the old no-menclature to designate the institutions which were being substi-tuted for the former ones in the new community. Reasons of prudence and tactfulness kept the community from using that terminology. But since it is almost natural that every society have some kind of "elders", these reasons would not have been a mo-tive with respect to introducing the term "presbyters".

Like the elders of Israel, the presbyters of the Christian com-munity in Jerusalem were members of the leading body of the community. One could object that the real leading body of the community was constituted by the twelve. This is true, but at the same time we would point out that the presbyters seem to appear among the leaders of the community just as the company of the twelve was itself being split up. The persecution of Agrippa I had reduced the twelve to ten: James, the brother of John, had been killed,[8] and Peter had left the community, *ad tempus*.[9] It seems safe to suppose that several of the apostles had left Jerusalem

---

[7] O. Seesemann, *Die Ältesten im Alten Testament* (Leipzig, 1895); J. McKenzie, "The Elders in the Old Testament," in *Studia Biblica et Orientalia* (Rome, 1959), pp. 388-406; J. van der Ploeg, "Les Anciens dans l'Ancien Testament," in *Lex Tua Veritas, Festschrift N. Junker* (Trier, 1961), pp. 175-91; cf. M. Guerra y Gomez, *op. cit.*, pp. 175-236.

[8] Acts 12, 1.

[9] Acts 12, 17.

after that persecution. Thus, it is also a plausible hypothesis to place the origin of the body of presbyters during the intermediate period of the martyrdom of James, the departure of Peter from Jerusalem and the celebration of the Council. Precisely in this period of time do we find mention of their existence in Jerusalem.[10] In fact, with James they gradually take over the place of the apostles themselves in Jerusalem. It is certain that several years later St. Paul finds only James and the presbyters at Jerusalem.[11]

(b) *The Presbyteral Colleges outside of Jerusalem*

Up to this point we have limited the discussion to the presbyters of Jerusalem; now we shall speak of the others. Paul and Barnabas established presbyters in the communities that arose during their first voyage.[12] The Acts give a clear account of this. It seems that the author of the Acts, in pointing out these facts, wanted to say that Paul and Barnabas meant to set up leaders in the new communities by these appointments.

The Acts also speak repeatedly of other presbyters. Returning from his third voyage Paul sent for the presbyters of the community at Ephesus.[13] These are presented as a body of presbyters —*episcopoi,* appointed by the Holy Spirit to shepherd the Church of God.[14] As *episcopoi* they must shepherd and nourish the flock, that is, they must arouse, corroborate and efficiently maintain in the members of the flock that life brought to them by Christ and conferred on them by means of the presbyters' teaching and baptism. Paul does not hesitate to ask the Lord to aid them so that they might always edify and raise up heirs among the sanctified.[15] If we wished to summarize the salient features of the presbyters' ministry at Ephesus, I think we might specify them thus: they appear as a college, especially as pastors and teachers of the faith.

The same pattern of duties, principally presbyter-teachers, is

[10] Acts 11, 27-30.
[11] Acts 21, 17ff.
[12] Acts 14, 23.
[13] Acts 20, 17ff.
[14] Acts 20, 28.
[15] Acts 20, 32.

characteristic of the presbyteral colleges established in Crete. Each presbyter-bishop is a steward of God. He must exhort in sound doctrine, reprove those who contradict it, and be vigilant for heterodox teachings.[16]

The first letter of Peter is even more explicit about the pastoral mission of the presbyteral colleges: "Tend the flock of God that is your charge, not by constraint but willingly . . . being examples to the flock." [17]

Another function of the college of presbyters is found in the letter of James: they shall lay hands on the sick. We get the impression that the presbyters are assigned to such a task, as it were, in imitation of Jesus who, in healing the sick, initiated a kind of pre-redemption.[18]

Finally, the presbyterium exercised power in sacred matters: the imposition of hands on Timothy.[19]

What precedents inspired Paul and Barnabas, and later Paul alone, to establish presbyters in their Churches?

It seems to me that these are the probable factors: in establishing the presbyters, Paul and Barnabas were thinking of the Judaic institutions of Palestine[20] and the Diaspora.[21] Further, they were inspired by the presbyteral institution of the Christian community in Jerusalem. These two precedents are very probable. But it is also probable that both of them on the first voyage, and then Paul alone on the following ones, also had an eye on the Hellenistic institution.[22]

We have mentioned that the presbyters of some colleges are also called *episcopoi;* the exercise of their office is sometimes indicated with the word *episcopein.* The problem has been the object of both old and recent studies. I have given my own conclusions in another work to which I can only refer here; it would not be

---

[16] Tit. 1, 5.
[17] 1 Pet. 5, 2.
[18] Jas. 5, 14-16.
[19] 1 Tim. 4, 14.
[20] Cf. M. Guerra y Gomez, *op. cit.,* pp. 175-236.
[21] *Ibid.,* pp. 236-59.
[22] *Ibid.,* pp. 25-67.

possible even to summarize them now.[23] I would only remark that if one accepts a particular solution of the problem, it follows that there were two types of presbyteral colleges: one type composed of bishops and presbyters and another composed of presbyters alone. This will become clear in Ignatius. Consequently, all that we have said about the presbyteral colleges is understood with the reservations deriving from the diversity of structure.

II

PRESBYTERAL COLLEGES IN THE POST-APOSTOLIC GENERATION

At the time of Clement of Rome there was a college of presbyters in Corinth. Their office has a *leiturgia*[24] through which they serve the flock of God.[25] Clement testifies that these presbyters work in a holy manner and without blemish.[26] In the last analysis their institution goes back to the apostles, who also established a rule of succession.[27] The presbyters must be respected; a certain stability belongs to their office, especially since the members of the community have given a promising report of their work.[28]

The letters of Ignatius of Antioch, written several decades after Clement, are one of the principal sources of knowledge about the presbyteral colleges. The term *presbuteroi* and the collective *presbuterion* recur frequently in them.[29] The office of presbyters is seen especially under the collegial aspect of a group of ministers, *sunhedrion theou,* a senate of God standing around the bishop.[30] Ignatius writes that the presbyterium of Magnesia

[23] Cf. G. D'Ercole, *op. cit. supra,* footnote 1, pp. 44-59.
[24] Clement of Rome, *1 Cor.* 44, 4-6 (Funk, *Patres Apost.* I, 157).
[25] *Idem, 1 Cor.* 44, 3 (Funk I, 157).
[26] *Ibid.*
[27] *Idem, 1 Cor.* 44, 1-2 (Funk I, 155).
[28] *Idem, 1 Cor.* 44, 3 (Funk I, 157).
[29] Ignatius of Antioch, *Magn.* 2; 3, 1-2; 6, 1; 7, 1-2; 13, 1-2 (Funk I, 233; 235-237; 241); *Smyrn.* 5, 1; 12, 2 (Funk I, 283; 287); *Eph.* 2, 2; 4, 1; 20, 2 (Funk I, 215; 217; 231); *Phil.* 4; 7, 1 (Funk I, 267); *Trall.* 2, 2; 7, 2; 13, 2 (Funk I, 245; 247-249; 251).
[30] *Idem, Trall.* 2, 1 (Funk I, 245).

is a worthy spiritual crown for its bishop.[31] That of Ephesus is
united to the bishop like the cords to the harp.[32] It is completely
one with the bishop and with the deacons, just as it is one before
the altar.[33] Not only is it the bishop's crown, it is also subject to
him and an example of conformity to his will.[34] The presbyterium
of Magnesia, even though composed of men venerable with age,
is exemplary in its subjection to its own bishop, notwithstanding
the fact that he is a young man.[35] The presbyterium of Smyrna,
formed of worthy persons, is beloved by God.[36] That of Ephesus
is likewise memorable and loved by God.[37] But if the presbyterium owes submission to its bishop, others in turn owe it honor
and obedience as to the senate of God.[38]

Ignatius declares that he is ready to give his life for those who
are subject to the bishop, to the presbyters and to the deacons.[39]
The faithful must be perfect, subject in single-minded obedience
to the bishop and to the presbyterium. Just as, through partaking
of the eucharist, there is immortality and life eternal in God, he
says, so also is there sanctification where obedience prevails.[40]
Ignatius has a marvelous passage on the harmony of thought,
action, prayer and charity which must animate the Christian community united to the bishop and to the presbyters.[41] Let the
faithful live under the guidance of the bishop, presbyters and
deacons. May they be subject to the presbyterium as to the
apostles of Jesus Christ.[42] The obligation of obedience to the
bishop, to the presbyterium and to the deacons is gravely binding
in conscience.[43] The presbyters have been named according to

[31] *Idem, Magn.* 13, 1-2 (Funk I, 241).
[32] *Idem, Eph.* 4, 1 (Funk I, 217).
[33] *Idem, Phil.* 4 (Funk I, 267).
[34] *Idem, Eph.* 4, 1 (Funk I, 217).
[35] *Idem, Magn.* 3, 1-2 (Funk I, 233).
[36] *Idem, Smyrn.* 12, 2 (Funk I, 287).
[37] *Idem, Eph.* 4, 1 (Funk I, 217).
[38] *Idem, Trall.* 2, 1 (Funk I, 245).
[39] *Idem, Pol.* 6, 1 (Funk I, 293).
[40] *Idem, Eph.* 2, 2; 20, 2 (Funk I, 215; 231).
[41] *Idem, Magn.* 7, 1-2 (Funk I, 235).
[42] *Idem, Magn.* 13, 1-2 (Funk I, 241); *Trall.* 2, 2 (Funk I, 245);
Smyrn. 8, 1 (Funk I, 283).
[43] *Idem, Trall.* 7, 2 (Funk I, 247-249).

the Spirit of Christ. They have been stably placed in office according to his will by means of the Holy Spirit.[44] They have a hierarchical place subordinate to the bishop.[45] After the bishop and with the deacons, the presbyters are essential components of the community. Without them one cannot speak of Church.[46]

Polycarp also describes the presbyters as a college which, with the bishop and the deacons, is at the head of the community.[47] He describes the office and the talents demanded of them: the presbyters must be ready to give compassion and mercy to everyone. Let them visit the sick, assist the widows, orphans and poor, and always be solicitous for good before God and men.[48]

Among the later Fathers who speak of presbyters are Papias,[49] Hermas,[50] Irenaeus,[51] Clement of Alexandria,[52] Origen[53] and Tertullian.[54] For the purpose of discussing the presbyteral colleges, the texts from these Fathers have no special importance. As a matter of fact, Papias and Irenaeus almost always designate bishops with the term "presbyters".

Another picture of the presbyteral college is apparent when the presbyters of Smyrna meet with Noetus and interrogate him with the dignified manner that an assembly of senators would have used. Because Noetus realized how much his faith differed from that of the Church, the presbyters interrogate him on several articles of the Creed. Noetus is obstinate. The presbyters do not discuss it, but expel him from the Church.[55]

We know of other presbyteral colleges in the letters of St.

[44] *Idem, Phil.* (preface) (Funk I, 265).
[45] *Idem, Magn.* 3, 1-2 (Funk I, 233).
[46] *Idem, Trall.* 2, 1 (Funk I, 245).
[47] Polycarp, *Phil.* (preface) (Funk I, 297).
[48] *Idem, Phil.* 6, 1 (Funk I, 203).
[49] Papias, *Fr.* 1, 1; 2, 3-4 (Funk I, 346; 351).
[50] Hermas, *Past. vis.* 2, 4, 3 (Funk I, 431).
[51] Irenaeus, *Adv. haer.* 4, 26, 2; 2, 22, 5.
[52] Clement of Alexandria, *Strom.* 7, 1 (*Patr. Graec.* 9, 405-406).
[53] Origen, *Hom. in Io.* 16, 2; *Is.* 6, 3; *Gen.* 4, 4; *Comm. in Matt.* 12, 24; *In Rom.* 8, 10; *Ex. in Ps.* 3, hom. 4, 3; *Fr. in Cant.* 3 (*P.G.* 12, 907; 13, 241-242; 12, 186; 13, 1616-1617, 1629; 14, 1188-1190; 12, 1385; 13, 149; *Corpus Berol.* 30, 396; 33, 272-273; 29, 54; 38, 18; 38, 40; 33, 176).
[54] Tertullian, *De baptismo* 17 (*Corp. Script. Eccl. Lat.* 20, 214).
[55] *Acta Archelai* 39 (*P.G.* 10, 1492).

Cyprian. The first part of these letters concerns in a special way the relations between the bishop, the presbyters, the other members of the clergy, the faithful and the confessors. The first thing to point out in these letters is the declaration of St. Cyprian that from the beginning of his episcopacy he made for himself a rule to do nothing without first having informed the presbyters and the deacons.[56] The affairs he considers are: the government of the Church of Carthage by the presbyters when the bishop is absent;[57] the conduct of confessors for the eucharistic celebration, with special admonitions to the presbyters who are told to celebrate individually, without the faithful in attendance, in order to avoid assemblies;[58] the nomination of several members of the clergy;[59] the norms to be carried out for assigning penance to those who have fallen away, and for their return in peace; the admonition to the presbyters to instruct the people in these matters and to fulfill the prescribed norms for their peaceful return; finally, the excommunication of several rebellious and schismatic presbyters.[60] Since the schism in the presbyteral college could compromise St. Cyprian's communion with other bishops, he is careful also to inform the episcopacy.[60a] Finally, inasmuch as the episcopal See of Rome is vacant, Cyprian writes to the presbyteral college there.

This Roman presbyteral college had already sent a letter expressing its opinion about the discipline to be adopted for fallen-aways.[61] For his part St. Cyprian shows a particular concern for solidarity with the presbyteral college of Rome. Thus, as was his custom, he sends those presbyters a series of documents with which he demonstrated his compliance with their opinion in questions of discipline.[62] For their part the Roman presbyters inform Cyprian that they had already written about this matter

[56] Cyprian, *Ep.* 14, 4 (*C.S.E.L.* 3, 2, 511).

[57] *Idem, Ep.* 14, 2 (*C.S.E.L.* 3, 2, 512).

[58] *Idem, Ep.* 5, 2 (*C.S.E.L.* 3, 2, 479).

[59] *Idem, Eph.* 29, 38; 39; 40 (*C.S.E.L.* 3, 2, 548; 579-586).

[60] *Idem, Eph.* 11; 14; 15-19; 26; 29; 33; 34; 37; 41; 43 (*C.S.E.L.* 3, 2, 495-502; 512-524; 539-540; 545-548; 566-571; 587-597).

[60a] Cf. G. D'Ercole, *op. cit. supra*, footnote 5, pp. 171-200.

[61] Cyprian, *Ep.* 8 (*C.S.E.L.* 3, 2, 485-488).

[62] *Idem, Eph.* 20; 27; 35 (*C.S.E.L.* 3, 2, 527-529; 540-544; 571-572).

in Sicily. They add that they consider it opportune to hold a general consultation in order to decide the problem of the fallen-aways. It should be noticed that the Roman presbyters always make their proposals with the reservation that they are subject to their future bishop for definitive solutions. In one of their letters the presbyteral college of Rome clearly affirms the obligation that they also have, because of the communion, to watch over the entire body of the Church.[63]

Thus, the letters of St. Cyprian are pertinent to our study. Here we see two presbyteral colleges, both of which are operating under exceptional circumstances. It is a regrettable situation since first the presbyteral college of Carthage and later that of Rome are disrupted when some of their members sever themselves from their own bishop.[64]

III

PROFOUND ALTERATION OF COLLEGIALITY
IN THE POST-APOSTOLIC AGE

If we ask again who were the ministers who had the power to celebrate the eucharist, we will see that the sources, beginning with Ignatius of Antioch until the time of St. Cyprian, and precisely until the persecution of Decius, give us texts on this question that demand the most attentive examination.

[63] *Idem, Ep.* 30; 36 (*C.S.E.L.* 3, 2, 549-556; 572-575).
[64] *Idem, Eph.* 59, 1-2. 9-11. 14. 16 (*C.S.E.L.* 3, 2, 666-667; 676-679; 683; 685)); *Eph.* 49; 50 (*C.S.E.L.* 3, 2, 608-614); W. Seston, "Note sur les origines des paroisses rurales," in *Rev. Hist. et Phil. rel.* (1935), pp. 243-54; G. Huard, "Considérations sur l'histoire de la paroisse rurale dès origines à la fin du Moyen Age," in *Revue d'histoire de l'Eglise de France* (1938), pp. 5ff.; J. Colson, "Fondement d'une spiritualité pour le prêtre de second rang," in *Nouv. Rev. Théol.* 73 (1951), pp. 1059ff.; A Roguet, "La collégialité du sacerdoce," in *Pastorale oeuvre commune* (Paris, 1956), pp. 128-43; B. Botte, "Presbyterium et ordo episcoporum," in *Irénikon* 29 (1956), p. 11; P. Dupont, "Collégiales et collégialité presbyterale," in *Le Courrier de Mondage* 46-47 (1956), pp. 8ff.; B. Botte, "Caractère collégial du presbyterat et de l'épiscopat," in *Etudes sur le sacrement de l'Ordre* (Paris, 1957); B. Batazole, "L'évêque et la vie chrétienne au sein de l'Eglise locale, dans Y. Congar—B. Dupuy," in *L'épiscopat et l'église universelle* (Paris, 1962).

Ignatius writes: "Let that eucharist be considered valid which is celebrated by the bishop or by someone whom he appoints. . . . Without the bishop it is impossible either to baptize or to celebrate the agape. Since everything he approves is pleasing to God, and so that everything that takes place be efficacious and valid . . . take care to use only one eucharist . . . only one altar with only one bishop, the presbyterium and the deacons. He who is in the altar is pure. He who is outside the altar is rather impure: that is, he who acts without the bishop, the presbyterium and the deacons is not clean in conscience.[65]

Reading these and other texts of Ignatius, one has the impression that only the bishop was the ordinary celebrant of the eucharist, and that the part of the presbyterium in the celebration consisted solely in being the crown of the bishop as a senate, as the apostolic college.

The *Didascalia* gives us a similar picture. It says explicitly in regard to concelebration that the eucharistic sacrifice is reserved exclusively to the bishop, and the presbyters sit beside him.[66]

It has been said that in the beginning Christianity was a town religion.[67] In fact, we find that every town had its ecclesiastical organization with a complete cadre of bishop, presbyterium, deacons, etc. The clearest example is that of Africa.[68]

But we can ask: Who celebrated when the bishop was prevented or was absent, or when the See was vacant? We find an answer in Ignatius. He says that another could celebrate the eucharist with the permission of the bishop. Ignatius does not specify who this other might be, but we think it was one of the presbyters.

Other indications are seen in Justin and Origen. Justin says that the eucharist was celebrated by a *proestoos*.[69] I believe that *proestoos* could be a presbyter as well as the bishop: ordinarily

---

[65] Ignatius of Antioch, *Smyrn.* 8, 2; *Phil.* 4, 1; *Trall.* 7, 2 (Funk I, 283; 267; 247-249).

[66] *Didasc.* 2, 26, 7; 2, 57, 3-4 (Funk, *Didasc.* 104, 1, 158-160).

[67] Cf. A. Harnack, *Missione e propagazione del Cristianesimo* (Torino, 1906), pp. 371-542.

[68] *Ibid.*, pp. 534ff.

[69] Justin Martyr, *Apol.* 1, 67 (*Patr. Lat.* 6, 1568).

the bishop, by exception a presbyter. Besides, Origen writes explicitly that the presbyter possessed the power to make the offering.[70]

It is clear that the permanence of the presbyteral colleges in the period of Christian origins was connected with this type of organization in the local Churches. But it is exactly in this period that new factors appear.

During the persecution of Decius, Cyprian makes provisions for the celebration of the eucharistic sacrifice by presbyters. They are to celebrate alone, assisted only by a deacon, in order to escape notice and apprehension by the police.[71] This is clearly an exceptional provision, but its importance for the history of the presbyteral colleges is enormous. If the presbyters begin to celebrate singly, the type of presbyteral organization which had existed until that time will no longer be the only type. The presbyters could even be sent off on their own to certain Christian centers. In fact, one begins to find the figure of the presbyter who exercises his ministry alone in isolated centers away from the cities. We find a well-known example in the narration of the dispute between Archelaus and Manes:[72] a presbyter exercising his ministry alone in a small center.

Even after the discipline has been greatly changed, we still find clear traces of the distant influence of the ancient discipline: in the custom of celebrating only one eucharist on Sunday, still observed in the 4th century, for example, in Milan and Carthage;[73] in the prescriptions of numerous councils that the presbyters return to the episcopal city for certain feasts and take part in the bishop's Mass;[74] and, finally, in the Roman practice of sending the fermentum to the titular presbyters.[75]

[70] Origen, *In Num., hom.* 2, 1.
[71] Cyprian, *Ep.* 5, 2 (*C.S.E.L.* 3, 2, 479).
[72] *Acta Archelai* 39 (*P.G.* 10, 1566).
[73] Ambrose, *Ep.* 20, 4-5 (*P.L.* 16, 1037); cf. V. Monachino, *La cura pastorale a Milano, Cartagine e Roma nel secolo IV* (Rome, 1947), pp. 54-55, 186; cf. C. De Smedt, "L'organisation des églises chrétiennes," in *Revue des quest. hist.* 43 (1888), pp. 329-84; 50 (1891), pp. 597ff.; J. Parisot, "Concélébration," in *Rev. Hist. et Litt. rel.* 2 (1898), pp. 97ff.
[74] Cf. B. Botte, *op. cit.,* p. 11.
[75] Cf. V. Monachino, *op. cit.,* p. 350.

CONCLUSIONS

First of all, the collegiality of the presbyters is part of the organic structure of the People of God both in the Old Testament and in the New Testament. However, in the Old Testament only the whole Israel is the People of God. Thus, if in addition to the institution one desires to designate an assembly with this name, only Israel organized in all its units and assembled as a whole in a single place (e.g., in the desert) can be called the People of God. The cities or single villages cannot be called the People of God in this sense. Christian terminology will differ in this respect.

In the early Christian writings every local Church can be called *ekklesia tou theou* and every local Church is the Church of God *paroikousa* in pilgrimage.[76]

I would consider this to be the deeper meaning of Ignatius' expression: only one Church, only one altar, only one bishop, only one presbyterium with the deacons; if one of these elements is missing the Church is not Church.[77]

Every Church of God is an individual sacramental community with the bishop at its head. He is the ordinary minister of the sacraments, and he is assisted by the presbyterium and the deacons. It is a community individual in its government, ruled by the bishop with the assistance of the presbyters and deacons. It is a community of faith, in unity of doctrine; this doctrine is taught especially by the presbyter-teachers.

Later conciliar legislation prohibited the erection of new bishoprics in those places where a single presbyter could suffice (the famous struggle against duplicate Sees).[78] Thus, there arose a practical criterion, different from the primitive one, for the distribution of presbyters in the Churches. We would like to point out one of the consequences of such new discipline: When only the more archaic structure was followed, a greater propriety of terminology was possible. Then, each place, every community,

[76] Mart. Pol., *Preface* (Funk I, 315).
[77] Ignatius of Antioch, *Trall.* 3, 1 (Funk I, 245).
[78] Council of Sardica, c. 6.

was complete with all its units. It was established in a single See, and thus truly the assembly of the People of God, *ekklesia tou theou*. It was not split up into those minor subdivisions which, when they arose, included only a part of the People of God and only some of its ministers.

Mario Rosa / *Bari, Italy*

Italian Jansenism and the Synod of Pistoia

The Movement for the Reform of the
Liturgy, Devotion, Canon Law, etc.,
Culminating in the Synod of Pistoia

I

PROFILE OF ITALIAN JANSENISM
AND NEW DIRECTIONS IN RESEARCH

From the end of the 18th century and throughout the 19th
century there was a long period of polemics concerning Italian
Jansenism. However, in the first fifty years of this century there
has been a more careful historiographic investigation. This in
turn has opened up a heated debate concerning the diverse
hypotheses and interpretations that have been proposed, especially those of E. Rota, A. C. Jemolo and E. Codignola. It is
not possible here to indicate the new editions of various unedited
material, particularly in the form of letters, or even the major
or minor contributions to the discussion. There has recently appeared a good review of the results attained through the evolution
of religious and ideological-political thought, which themselves
have periodically been subjected to fruitful research. We would
refer anyone who wishes to reexamine this aspect of the problem
to this study.[1]

However, we want to point out specifically the studies of E.

[1] F. Margiotta Broglio, "Appunti storiografici sul giansenismo italiano,"
in *Raccolta di scritti in onore di Arturo Carlo Jemolo* I, 2 (Milan, 1962),
pp. 791-849.

Passerin d'Entrèves,[2] since they are connected more immediately with our reconstruction of the factors that culminated in the reformist activities of Scipione de' Ricci and the Synod of Pistoia (1786). The studies of Passerin have shed light on the tone, the subtle ties, the convergences and divergences of a complex reform movement directed at ecclesiastical life and permeating the political and religious orientations of the late 18th century in Italy.[3] Passerin situates all this against the background of enlightened despotism and, in particular, the ecclesiastical politics of the Grand Duke of Tuscany, Peter Leopold.

The more conspicuously religious aspects of Jansenism in Tuscany are part of an atmosphere of jurisdictionalism and royalism characteristic of Tuscany under Peter Leopold. They are further imbedded in, and intermingled with, the general trends

[2] E. Passerin D'Entrèves, "Studi e problemi politico-religiosi dell'Italia del 700," in *Quaderni di cultura e storia sociale* 2 (1953), pp. 22-28; "La politica dei giansenisti in Italia nell'ultimo Settecento," *ibid.*, 2-3 (1953-54); "Corrispondenze francesi relative al Sinodo di Pistoia del 1786," in *Rev. di storia della Chiesa in Italia* 7 (1953), pp. 377-410, and 8 (1954), pp. 49-92; "Il fallimento dell'offensiva riformista di Scipione de' Ricci secondo nuovi documenti (1781-1788)," *ibid.*, 9 (1955), pp. 99-131; "L'istituzione dei Patrimoni ecclesiastici e il dissidio fra il vescovo Scipione de' Ricci ed i funzionari leopoldini (1783-1789)," in *Rassegna storica toscana* 1 (1955), pp. 6-27; "La riforma 'giansenista' della Chiesa e la lotta anticuriale in Italia nella seconda metà del Settecento," in *Riv. storica italiana* 71 (1959), pp. 209-34.

[3] After its ethical and theological flowering in the 17th century (St. Cyran, Pascal and Arnauld), French Jansenism was able to insert itself as a whole—with the polemics about *Unigenitus*—into the structure of the Gallican Church. Thus, on a political and ecclesiastical plane it could utilize the might of Parlement. By contrast, 18th-century Italian Jansenism, after a period marked by extensive effort to recover Augustianism, quickly passed from the plane of doctrinal discussions (especially 1740-60) through the anti-Jesuit controversy to a practical and disciplinary phase. This marked the end of the hopes for an internal reform of the Church, and the consolidation of the Enlightenment reformism. However, it came to assume extremely variable forms. It disclosed jurisdictionalistic aspects in Sabaudian Piedmont, courtly and governmental aspects in Austrian Lombardy, anticurial aspects and concern with devotional problems in the territories of Venice and Rome, royalist and episcopalist aspects in the kingdom of Naples. From the Jansenism of the Low Lands —toward which it showed a preference to gravitate in this, its latest period—it derived not theological preoccupations, but essentially disciplinary ones in sacramental matters and on the level of the ecclesiastical institution and, in general, the formidable canonistic framework.

common to ecclesiastical politics and the religious life of Europe in the 18th century.[4] Now, however, it is possible for us to re-examine Jansenism in Tuscany with the stimulus of perspectives opened up in the life of the Catholic Church by the discussions and the decisions of Vatican Council II. Some of these perspectives reveal an extraordinary agreement with the endeavors for, and the preoccupations with, reform in Tuscan Jansenism. The *Constitution on the Sacred Liturgy* (December 4, 1963) is a good example in its synthesis of an extensive contemporary movement of liturgical renewal and pastoral preoccupation.[5]

Although present preoccupation may stimulate historical interest in the study of the events and conditions of the past, it is nevertheless worthwhile to point out an important methodological principle. If research and interrogations of the past are to receive a legitimate response, the intention that inspires them must not affect the particular, concrete characterization of historical problems. These problems have meaning and are comprehended only from the situations, passions, struggles and ideals of their own time.

II

SCIPIONE DE' RICCI'S DEVOTIONAL
AND LITURGICAL REFORM ACTIVITIES

Catholic scholars (Jemolo, Matteucci, etc.) have judged the Synod of Pistoia (1786) quite disparagingly. Passerin d'Entrèves, on the other hand, reaches more sober conclusions. Nevertheless, the Synod was the final outcome of the whole movement of 18th-century Jansenism with its progressive episcopalistic and parochialistic radicalism. The proceedings of the Synod reflect as in a clouded mirror the travail of secular discussions and, nearer in time, the accomplishments of the years during which Ricci

[4] Cf. M. Rosa, "Giurisdizionalismo e riforma religiosa nella politica ecclesiastica leopoldina," in *Rassegna storica toscana* 11 (1965), pp. 257-300.

[5] Cf. J. Gelineau, "Réforme liturgique, renouveau de l'Eglise," in *Etudes* (1964), pp. 8-26.

was Bishop of Pistoia. The context of the Synod can be understood by referring to "Richer's Great Scheme":[6] diocesan convocations were to have led to individual national councils and finally to an ecumenical council. We can appreciate its background if we consider the example of the Church of Utrecht and its provincial Synod of 1763. One should also consider the *Fifty-seven Ecclesiastical Articles* which the Grand Duke Peter Leopold proposed to the bishops of Tuscany as a *magna charta* for the desired ecclesiastical reform of the State.

At the Synod itself the ideas of French Jansenism were present, and there were also direct representatives of various groups of Italian Jansenists. Tendencies that were sometimes even contradictory appeared for a moment and then again faded away. These tendencies were cemented together in Ricci's activism and radicalism, which were the chief elements enriching the various attitudes of 18th-century ecclesiastical and religious currents. Even prior to his *Memoirs,* Ricci presented a profile of his pastoral activity in the dioceses of Pistoia and Prato in a pastoral letter of 1787.[7] In this letter he emphasized the need of an "enlightened" piety. This rationalistic—if not directly illuministic—attitude and this intellectual vein always persisted in Bishop Ricci's thoughts, even when he seemed more religiously involved. To this end, he published the famous pastoral letter of 1781 against the "new" devotion to the Heart of Jesus, and he initiated the *Ordo Divini Officii* for the liturgical-devotional reform of the diocese of Pistoia—actions which brought him instantaneously into the spotlight of European Jansenism.

[6] From the name of the Gallican writer E. Richer (1559-1631), defender of Gallicanism in his book *Libellus de ecclesiastica et politica potestate.*

[7] *Lettera pastorale di mons. vescovo di Pistoia e Prato . . . stampata in Pistoia* dated 1787 . . . s.l. 1788. However, the reforming activity of Ricci has been reconstructed, particularly through the documents in the appendix of *Atti e decreti del Concilio diocesano di Pistoia dell'anno 1786* (Firenze, 1788 [2]), by means of the *Omilie de Monsignore Scipione de' Ricci* (Pistoia, 1788), by G. Marchetti, *Annotazioni pacifiche di un parroco cattolico . . .* s.l. (1788) (anti-Ricci), and by F. Guasco, *Dizionario ricciano e antiricciano* (Assisi, 1796 [3]) (also anti-Ricci, but valuable for its notations).

For a similar reason, in 1782 he presented the *Instruction on the Necessity and the Manner of Studying Religion* which draws upon a similar Instruction from the Jansenistic Archbishop of Lyon, Montazet. This contained in a nutshell the fundamental points of his program: the polemic against superficial catechetical instruction (whence the problem of the catechism—a central issue for 18th-century Jansenism—and the substitution of the Roman catechism by that of Gourlin, accompanied by scripture readings in the translations of Sacy and Mésenguy, and by the church history of Racine); the exhortation to a deep participation of the faithful in the charismatic life of the Church; the renewal of a rigorous penitential discipline; a univocal conception of the ecclesial mystical body; enthusiasm for a reinvigoration of the primary community ties symbolized in the parish bond.

In the same year, 1782, Ricci sent a letter to pastors, together with the *Via Crucis* written by a Venetian Benedictine, Puiati. This "new" Franciscan devotion spread with surprising rapidity in 18th-century Italy through the work of St. Leonard of Porto Maurizio. Bishop Ricci did not reject it, but he wanted to "moderate" it with a particular christocentric sensitivity.

The year 1783 was of central importance for a broadening of horizons in Ricci's own program. On April 11, he presented an Instruction of the Archbishop of Salzburg, Colloredo, dated June 29, 1782. This had been forwarded to him by the Grand Duke; it was inspired by the "katholische Aufklärung" of Joseph II and by the "moderated devotion" of Muratori. The principal themes of the document are simplicity in Church decorations, severity in ecclesiastical music, devout hymns in the national language, "moderated devotion" to the saints, "moderated" interpretation of indulgences, and scriptural readings. These initiatives in the diocese of Pistoia were to lead practically to the reorganization of ecclesiastical functions: henceforth, they must be characterized by the greatest simplicity. They led also to the suppression of novenas, triduums, privileged altars and indulgences, to "moderated devotion" to the saints and Marian piety, the uncovering of veiled holy images, a different arrangement of relics, a new penitential system and emphasis on the eucharistic cult.

On January 1, 1786, Ricci presented the new breviary to his pastors. It contained changes in the antiphons and hymns and especially in the lessons, as well as a drastic reduction in the proper of the saints, so that the reading of scripture and the Sunday office would be placed in full relief. In addition to the breviary, Ricci also announced radical reforms of the ritual and the missal which were to be worked out by the coming Synod. In this connection, words of moderation were sent to him by the "Friends of France", a group gathered around the journal *Nouvelles ecclésiastiques;* this advice concerned especially the introduction of the vernacular in the administration of the sacraments and in the celebration of the Mass. The use of Italian, according to the suggestions offered in the pastoral letter of Colloredo, would be directed for the time being in a purely devotional sense with the translation of the *Pange lingua* and of Psalm 119.[8] However, a tradition in this direction already existed in Pistoia, at least tendentiously. Ricci's predecessor had been the rigorist Bishop Ippoliti who had leanings toward Jansenism. Ippoliti had recommended the recitation of the *Our Father* and the *Hail Mary* in Italian (which Ricci was to alter with a Jansenistic accent)[9] and caused hymns and prayers to be printed in the vernacular and the *Miserere* to be sung in Italian. Besides, similar inclinations based on Muratori had existed to a greater or lesser degree for at least forty years in many dioceses of Tuscany.

Only after the Synod, which decided on a delaying tactic, as we shall see, did Ricci attempt radical innovations in the liturgical sphere. He allowed Mass to be celebrated in Italian in some churches of the diocese, and he permitted two laymen to sing the *Passio* in Italian on Good Friday, 1787. But these were to be the extreme limits of his reforms. On the liturgical-devotional

[8] *Atti e decreti* . . . *op. cit. supra,* footnote 7, *Appendice* n. VII, pp. 8-10.

[9] For example, he translated *Panem nostrum quotidianum da nobis hodie* by *Dacci oggi il pane nostro soprassostanziale* (our supersubstantial bread), and *Ne nos inducas in tentationem* by *Signore, non ci abbandonate nella tentazione* (do not abandon us in temptation).

plane his reforms, stimulated purely by a new sense of the liturgy, were pointed more in the devotional direction. Within this historical profile of 18th-century piety as inspired by rigoristic Jansenism, it would be worthwhile to analyze the devotional writings of the small prayer manuals that Ricci placed in the hands of the faithful during this period:[9a] *Short Prayers for Parish Use, The Method of Prayer and Assistance at Holy Mass according to the Intention of the Church, Short Prayers for the Use of Christian Families,* and *Exercises of Christian Virtues,* which is an extract from the *Réflexions* of Quesnel,[10] edited by the Neopolitan Jansenist, Simioli. All these works were small compilations intended to encourage, within the sphere of the parish community, the direct participation of the faithful in the liturgy and common prayer.

III

RICCI'S IDEA OF THE RELATIONS BETWEEN
LITURGY AND ECCLESIOLOGY

The problem of the meaning of the parish and of the functions and responsibilities of the pastor is intimately connected with the liturgical-devotional renewal desired by Ricci. However, this problem developed gradually and autonomously until it became a determining and commanding influence in the development of his reformism. This motive, already mentioned in the instructions and the letters of 1782 and 1783, penetrated the entire *Pastoral Letter on the Erection of New Parishes in Prato* (January 6, 1784). This appeared in 1783 after the organization of the ecclesiastical patrimonies for the dioceses of Pistoia and Prato under the pressure of Ricci and encouraged by Grand Duke Peter Leopold. The works of Richer, Maultrot, Le Gros, Cornaro and the Brescian Jansenist Guadagnini provided the theoretical genesis of Ricci's "parochialism". Its practical models were to

---

[9a] *Brevi preghiere ad uso delle parrocchie, Maniera di pregare e di assistere alla S. Messa secondo l'intenzione della Chiesa, Brevi preghiere ad uso delle famiglie cristiane, Esercizi di virtù cristiane.*

[10] A Jansenist theologian, born in Paris (1634-1719).

be found in Joseph II's "good pastor" and in the suggestions of Peter Leopold for the formation of "zealous and useful" ecclesiastics. However, the "parochialism" of Ricci, articulated in the Synod in a particular attempt at "ecclesiastical democracy", also derived from a new sense of eucharistic piety understood as the participation of the faithful with the priest in the value of the sacrifice. This opposed the individualistic accent on the spiritual benefit of the sacrament sanctioned by the post-Tridentine practice of "frequent communion".

Ricci desired to bridge the gap between the forms of worship, and the participation of the faithful in those forms. On the one hand, he wanted to eliminate or "moderate" supplementary devotions originally intended to increase individual piety but more often than not based on extra-liturgical acts. On the other hand, he sought to re-create the sense of community in liturgical actions and in prayer based on the primary nucleus of the faithful around the pastor. The latter was sought in the simplicity and transparency of the gestures of faith and the biblical and patristic preferences characteristic of rigorist and Jansenistic sentiment. In this way he clearly crossed the limits of individual prayer in order to restore the spiritually pregnant worth of "public worship".

Ricci's reforms found new propaganda weapons in the volumes of the famous *Collection of Works concerning Religion (Raccolta di opuscoli interessanti la Religione,* Pistoia, 1783-89). In order to understand this religious tension and the impetuous development of Ricci's reform, we must emphasize its confrontation with the Catholic Church and the ecclesiastical organization as they had taken shape through post-Tridentine institutionalism. We often see Ricci's explicit but ambiguous appeal to the Council of Trent. This reflects a typical motive of Jansenistic "conciliarism". But, above all, Ricci exhibits an anxiety for conflict, especially with the more evident expressions of Counter-Reformation Catholicism. In this light we see the precise meaning of his efforts for the diffusion and knowledge of scripture, both Old and New Testaments, among clergy and faithful as their primary spiritual nourishment. We can also better appreciate his view of the liturgy through a dynamic feeling for the Christian mystery and the attention he gives to the sacrificial and community value of the Mass, from which comes his insistence on liturgical communion *infra missam*. We should also see in this light his hostility toward the individualistic forms of the cult of Mary and the saints as these were found in popular piety, and, finally, his battle with the regular clergy and, in general, with all the particularistic forces and institutions that had ruptured the primary bond and unity of the parish (churches of the mendicant orders, public and private oratories, confraternities, clergy possessing benefices without the care of souls, etc.).

Thus, the most obvious tendency was concerned as a whole— by means of devotional and liturgical reforms and practical transformations of ecclesiastical discipline—with re-creating the broken bond of the community against a consolidated and crystallized hierarchical structure. However, this more profound sensitivity—profound in the sense of completely spiritual—of the ecclesial bond, in accordance with the Gallican and parochialist theories of Richer and the Josephite theories of Curalt, brought with it two consequences. On the one hand, there was a royalist accent which worked in various degrees into the hands of the secular power and State authorities with respect to the rights not merely *circa sacra* but *in sacra*—the old jurisdictionalism. Thus, the civil authority obtained rights over all those aspects of religious and ecclesiastical life which also involved social factors (church property, marriage, cult, formation and organization of the clergy). On the other hand, through a "horizontal" perspective of ecclesial organization, instead of a "vertical" one, there occurred the recovery of a sentiment which, if not lost, had certainly been mitigated in large measure in the historical and institutional evolution of the life of the Catholic Church from the medieval to the modern period.

This feeling of visible or invisible unity among the members of Christianity in reverence to the primal See was characteristic of Jansenistic "ecumenism". (One thinks of the letters of "communion" with the Church of Utrecht.) The Roman See was

granted only the prerogative of vigilance and a ministerial primacy
necessary for the maintenance of the unity of faith in the diversity
of discipline and liturgy. This view touched upon an ideal or
idealized moment of the Christian life. However, Ricci with one
leap jumped from the moment of Trent over the medieval period
of Scholasticism and the "false decretals"—what in his eyes was
a long period of obscurity and decadence—to the "venerable
antiquity", the "golden age" of primitive Christianity, the ap-
ostolic-patristic age. Ricci's feeling for antiquity had a religious
color, but at the same time it was set in the fabric of the Enlightenment. It was a return to the origins after which had come
degenerations and deformations. It was a return to a mythical
purity, to an ecclesiastical garb and a religious life according to
"the canons of the Fathers who were always the delight and the
decoration of better times. . . ." [11]

IV

THE SYNOD OF PISTOIA:
TOWARD THE JANSENISTIC REFORM OF THE CHURCH

As we have seen, the reformism of Ricci and the decrees of the
Synod of Pistoia assumed, to a certain extent, a composite character within this archaic framework.

From Febronius and Eybel came antiromanism and episcopalism, and from Richer, "parochialistic" tendencies. From the
Franco-Belgian (Launoy, Van Espen) and Josephite (Eybel,
Litta, Tamburini) quarters came the question of marriage dispensations. From discussions among Jansenistic groups in Lombardy and Naples came the polemic over communion *infra
missam* and the problem of the catechism. From Jansenism in
Liguria, and, in particular, Palmieri's *Treatise about Indulgences,*
they absorbed the criticism of indulgences. The attempts to
reform the breviary grew especially out of French Jansenism,

[11] *Lettera pastorale . . . con data del 1787 . . . , op. cit. supra,* footnote 7.

while the central inspirations for the liturgical reforms are to be found in Muratori's *Della regolata divozione* (On moderated devotion) and in the "katholische Aufklärung". The importance of the latter consisted precisely in its having transferred and diffused at the pastoral level what had been for the "maurini" and other scholars of the ancient occidental and oriental liturgies (from the end of the 17th century into the early 18th century) only a question of devout erudition, an historico-critical exigency, at the very most limited to monastic circles. The problem of the translation of scripture into the vernacular was taken over from French Jansenism. Ricci's own reformism added the bold desire to crown the action of reform in the Synod and to trace the prospective lines of a future national Tuscan Church.

Ricci assigned to Tamburini, the foremost theologian of Italian Jansenism, the difficult task of elaborating the decrees in the so-called intermediate congregations of the Synod. Tamburini's prowess is perhaps a result of his teaching at the University of Pavia and of the writings brought to maturity at the center of Josephite reformism. It is certain that these decrees were presented as an adaptation of the decrees of Trent; as Jemolo justly remarks, they were "the official expression of a new doctrine of faith". The decrees were discussed and approved between September 18 and September 28, 1786, by a number of "fathers" who varied in number between 234 and 244. We will consider only some of the decrees and the points which have more direct relevance to our discussion.

The first decree "on the faith and on the Church" (Sess. III) asserted the right of the faithful to resist irregular methods of blind obedience or decrees which do not reflect the voice of the universal Church. This, together with an appeal for tolerance— clearly under the influence of Tamburini who had accepted the Four Gallican Articles of 1682—disguised by means of a restructuring of the Church in a synodal-episcopal-parochial sense the decision to do away with the ecclesiastical structure and canonical edifice on which the "Roman" hierarchical structure was based.

The decrees on the sacraments in general (baptism, confirmation and the eucharist) were approved in Session IV. The second of these exhorted the utmost simplicity in the administration of baptism. In order to restore to pastors one of their principal functions, it was decreed that baptism was to be conferred exclusively in the parish.

The decree "on the eucharist" is also quite meaningful. The Synod exhorted pastors to present the mystery according to the Fathers of the Church. It renewed the ancient canons prescribing the reservation only of consecrated hosts necessary for the sick and in cases of grave necessity. It declared its wish to maintain as a pious religious usage the feast of Corpus Christi which had already been regulated by Ricci in 1785. But in order to increase the respect and veneration of the blessed sacrament, the Synod recommended "the restoration of the practice of exposing it in the monstrance and carrying it in public procession only during the octave of Corpus Christi. The custom of exposing [the blessed sacrament] only once a month in the Cathedral Church is to be retained". In confirmation of the liturgical-devotional reforms of Ricci, the Synod resolved to substitute the litanies of our Lord in Italian for those usually recited in honor of the saints during the eucharistic adoration.[12]

In the main part of the decree enjoining the participation of the faithful in the sacrifice, the Synod recommended that the celebrants recite all the words of the rite "distinctly and devoutly" (an implicit reference to the celebrated Jansenistic thesis on reading the canon of the Mass aloud). It rigorously forbade organ music during the most important part of the sacrifice, from the offertory to the postcommunion. It decreed that the blessed sacrament should be reserved in ciboria in an elevated place, thus renewing an ancient custom. Any paintings not having reference to the eucharist were to be removed from the place of reservation. Furthermore, in harmony with a reform that Ricci had already carried out here and there, it was decided to restore the practice of having only one altar in each church. Thus, the inconveniences

[12] *Atti e decreti, op. cit. supra,* footnote 7, *Appendice* n. VII, pp. 6-8.

of simultaneous celebration of several Masses were eliminated and the fervor of the faithful community was united in a single sacrifice.

In defining the liturgical aspects of the sacrifice, the Synod declared its propensity to suppress all those factors by which the actions themselves had lost their original value as participation, "by recalling the liturgy to a greater simplicity of rites, by explaining it in the vernacular language, and by reciting it in a loud voice". However, considering the impossibility of an immediate reform, the Synod restricted itself to recommending the explanation of a portion of the liturgy of the Mass and the distribution among the faithful of small missals written in Italian. Nevertheless, deeming the sharing of the victim as an essential part of the sacrifice, the Synod obliged priests to give communion to the faithful *infra missam* in consideration of "the particular fruit which comes from liturgical communion".

Session V saw the approval of decrees on penance, extreme unction, orders and matrimony. The first-mentioned was a polemic against attrition and casuistry; it returned to the penitential discipline expressed in the *Pastor bonus* of Opstraet and in the recommendation of St. Charles Borromeo. However, the form of absolution itself was profoundly altered by suppressing as "modern" part of the formula to be accompanied, according to the ancient discipline, by the imposition of hands on the penitent. The current teaching about indulgences was also substantially revised. In suppressing all indulgences, and in particular those applicable to the deceased, the Synod prescribed that confessors should apply them solely according to the ancient principle of absolution from canonical penalties. The decree concluded with three reforms that were inserted like a wedge in the body of the discipline. It confirmed the faculty delegated to pastors by Ricci for the absolution of reserved cases. It rejected the excommunication *ipso facto incurrenda*. It declared invalid all unjust excommunications, in accordance with a theme that had become traditional in the course of the polemic around *Unigenitus*. The suspension of priests *ex informata conscientia* was likewise declared invalid and contrary to the natural right and the paternal practice of episcopal authority.

The decree on extreme unction treated this sacrament as the complement of the sacrament of penance, in accordance with the constant practice of all the Churches until the 13th century and still maintained in some Churches in France. The Synod exhorted the administration of this sacrament to the sick before the eucharist.

The decree on orders confirmed the will of the Synod to destroy the system of benefices and to heal the sore caused by the distinction between order and benefice. This had arisen from a pseudo-Isidorian and erroneous interpretation of a decree of the Lateran Synod of Alexander III. The Synod saw an effective remedy for the abuses created by medieval canonical procedure in the institution of the ecclesiastical patrimony. This would make the entire diocesan clergy active and productive by means of adequate recompenses.

The decree on matrimony was truly central in the provisions of the Synod because of its declared intention of modifying the Tridentine canons in the direction of a conspicuously "civil" orientation. The contract was distinguished from the sacrament, and the secular power was to possess original and exclusive competence. In view of this, the Synod requested that the Grand Duke suppress or limit a series of diriment impediments and that he delegate the bishops to give the necessary dispensations. However, the decree aroused such a violent reaction on the part of the scanty minority that in the following Session VI the intermediate congregation was forced to reply. It is interesting to notice in the reply a contradistinction of Roman law and canon law and the affirmation of the superiority and hegemony of the first over the second. This recourse to Roman law as the primary source was a traditional tactic of the jurisdictionalists. Roman law was seen as an historical document which attested to the existence of a Church subject to the sovereign, a law competing with the other sources in defining the limits of the privileges of the Church itself. Nevertheless, precisely in its juridical argumentation, the debate reflected an essential moment in the relations between Church and State, and thus was connected with a vital problem in the consciousness of 18th-century society.

The decree on prayer (Session VI) had a completely different tone. The pastoral preoccupations of the Synod were presented in some of the most sublime pages, as regards religious depth, written by Italian Jansenism. Although it is scarcely germane with Italian Jansenism, there appeared in the decree the famous idea of Pascal that it is impossible for man to pray directly to God since the fall. There remains for man no other means by which he can approach God than the only-begotten Son: We "recognize his spirit that groans and prays in us; we ask for everything according to his will, and in the order of goods merited by him, we unite ourselves to his prayer and sacrifice, our sole mediator". However, more than from Pascal himself, these ideas are taken perhaps more directly from the work of the appellant Duguet and from Guibaud's *Gémissements d'une âme pénitente*. The latter had been circulated especially among the Jansenists of Liguria and Tuscany. However, into the light of this conception of prayer soon appeared the polemical motives proper to Ricci's reformism, namely, with respect to the cult of the saints and of Mary, and with respect to the completion of the liturgical-devotional reforms, etc. But the Synod went a step further, as if to cement the bonds of the community and the uniformity of prayer and religious instruction. It proposed that the pastors read Quesnel's *Réflexions,* the "golden book" which Ricci introduced on October 6, 1786, in Italian translation.

V

THE HISTORICAL SIGNIFICANCE OF AN UNDERTAKING

The national Council called for by the Synod of Pistoia was imminent. However, in 1787 the preparatory assembly of the bishops of Tuscany disposed of the undertaking. It was definitively condemned by Rome in the bull *Auctorem fidei* (August

28, 1794). The eighty-five propositions of this document strike formally at the Gallican and Richerian ecclesiology (prop. 1-15), at the theological foundations of Jansenism (prop. 16-26), and especially at the modifications of sacramental discipline and, in particular, penitential discipline (prop. 27-60) and at the liturgical-devotional reformism in general as this was projected or realized through Ricci's work and the synodal decrees (prop. 61-79). In this way Rome rejected in general the conclusions and the attempts of Ricci and the Synod of Pistoia to discern simply elements of corruption and decadence in the historical evolution of ecclesiastical discipline and institutions, as well as in the evolution of liturgy and piety. Rome thus rejected the attempt to bind the reforms to a historically individuated moment of the life of the Church mythically relived and polemically distinguished from other moments of the tradition.

Thus, the movement which was synthesized in the Synod of Pistoia was destined to failure. In this it followed the same path to the same conclusion as Leopold's reformism. Although bound to the fortunes of a political and ecclesiastical period, on the threshold of the Revolution and in a period of general crisis, it discloses dramatically just how rich Italian Jansenism really was in religious content and ferment. It was an urgent attempt to overcome a long period in the life of the Roman Church. It is a particular episode in an historical and ideal process which perhaps only in our own time—after the complex events in Catholicism during the last century and the first half of this century— can be said to be definitively concluded.

Johannes Van Laarhoven/*Nijmegen, Netherlands*

The Origin of Luther's Doctrine of the Two Kingdoms

Ever since the appearance, just after World War II, of Karl Barth's stringent criticism of Luther's error regarding the relationship between secular and spiritual power —an error which may have resulted in the ideological strengthening of paganism in Germany—there has been a steady flow of books and articles both for and against Luther's doctrine of the two kingdoms.[1] The Swiss theologian's recent self-criticism, in which he says that he has become more "comprehensive",[2] may be construed as mollifying his criticism of Luther. But it is clear from the subsequent debate that he touched a sensitive nerve in the Protestant view of the Christian in the world. The revival of Protestant interest in this problem has to a remarkable extent been concurrent with Catholic interest in the relationship be-

[1] K. Barth, *Eine Schweizer Stimme 1938-1945* (Zürich, 1945), p. 113; cf. J. van den Berg, *Twee regimenten, één Heer* (Kampen, 1961), pp. 5-6, 27-8. For a bibliography of the doctrine of the two kingdoms in Luther, see the articles by P. Althaus and J. Heckel in *Evangelisches Kirchenlexikon* III (1959), pp. 1945-7; this information has now been supplemented by L. Schuurman's Amsterdam dissertation, *Confusio regnorum. Studie zu einem Thema aus Luthers Ethik* ('s-Gravenhage, 1965). A historical survey of the theme of the two kingdoms (together with bibliography) was provided by G. Kretschmar in "Die zwei Imperien und die zwei Reiche," in *Ecclesia und Res Publica* (Göttingen, 1961), pp. 89-112.

[2] K. Barth, "Reformierte Theologie in der Schweiz," in *Ex auditu Verbi. Theologische opstellen aangeboden aan G. Berkouwer* (Kampen, 1965), pp. 27-36, esp. p. 34.

tween the Church and the world. To try to squeeze Luther into Schema 13 would hardly seem to be of any benefit to the ecumenical cause, but an investigation into the background of his doctrine of the two kingdoms may help to shed light on a problem that is specifically neither Catholic nor Protestant, but characteristically Christian.

LUTHER'S TWO KINGDOMS

In several occasional writings, Luther discussed our position as Christians in the world, dealing with such topics as our attitude toward law, authority, the organization of society, work and marriage. Any attempt to summarize his answers systematically is in itself a risky undertaking, but some kind of resumé is in order as a point of departure.[3]

Humanity is divided into believers and unbelievers, each group forming a *corpus,* which is not visible as such in society. Both groups are subject to a head: one kingdom is subject to Christ, while the other, to use a frequent phrase of Luther himself, is "a kingdom of the evil one", a *corpus diaboli.* The two kingdoms are at war with each other until the final victory of Christ, who then hands one kingdom over to the Father. This, then, is the fundamental significance of the doctrine of the two kingdoms.[4]

This scheme, however, is determined by the so-called "doctrine of the regiment", and Luther himself frequently used such terms as *regnum, regiment, Gewalt, Bereich, Kirche* and *Christenheit* without making any precise distinction among them. "Regiment" primarily refers to the mode of God's rule, the manner in which God the creator governs his creatures in the world. The regiment can be considered the *modus quo,* whereas the kingdom is the

---

[3] An excellent summary is provided by H. Bornkamm, "Luthers Lehre von den zwei Reichen im Zusammenhang seiner Theologie," in *Archiv für Reformationsgeschichte* 49 (1958), pp. 26-49 (also separately: Gütersloh, 1958). Cf. also the different approach by Althaus and Heckel, *op. cit.,* footnote 1, pp. 1928-45.

[4] J. Heckel, "Im Irrgarten der Zwei-Reiche-Lehre," in *Theologische Existenz heute,* New Series, 55 (Munich, 1957), p. 6.

locus quo or the *effectum quod*. God works in Christ spiritually, inwardly and through his Word, which confers grace and evokes faith in the hearts of those who thereby become members of the spiritual kingdom. But God's omnipotence is also outwardly and corporally effective through the rod of correction and the sword of authority—in short, through force—with those who do not believe and who thereby become members of the worldly kingdom. God is thus active in both kingdoms, his will being present through the regiments of his right and his left hands.[5]

The war between God and the devil is waged in the worldly kingdom, and not in the spiritual kingdom where everything is grace, peace and freedom because Christ, who is everything, is there. Conflict, suffering, death and force—these form part of the worldly kingdom. The cunning of the evil one consists in allowing the members of his kingdom to be tempted to appropriate the spiritual kingdom; at the same time, the members of the spiritual kingdom are tempted to conquer the worldly kingdom, that is, to lay a claim to the dominion of the world. This double cunning gives rise to *confusio,* the confusion of both kingdoms, through which God's double activity is obscured and thwarted. Papists, baptists and all fanatics (*Schwärmer*) try, each in their own way, to tyrannize the world by so-called spiritual means. Similarly, many princes misuse their worldly power in the name of the spirit. Their attempts of both groups are instigated by the devil.[6]

One final aspect of this doctrine should also be taken into consideration. Whoever is under God's spiritual regiment in the spiritual kingdom lives there in the spirit of the Sermon on the Mount, as a person, *coram Deo*. At the same time, however, we live under God's worldly regiment, subject to the laws and ordinances of the worldly kingdom. But the Christian knows this, and that is the great difference between him and his fellowmen who

---

[5] Bornkamm, *op. cit.,* footnote 3, pp. 30-1 and 35-6.

[6] This is dealt with in detail in Schuurman, *op. cit.,* footnote 1, pp. 147-79 ("Die katholische Vermischung") and pp. 180-234 ("Die schwärmerische und obrigkeitliche Vermischung").

do not believe. He will therefore behave in the worldly kingdom as the doer of God's will and must appear *coram hominibus*.[7]

AUGUSTINE'S TWO CITIES

Where does this doctrine originate? It does, of course, contain echoes of the bible, but leaving these aside, anyone who encounters Luther's doctrine of the two kingdoms for the first time is bound to be reminded of Augustine's two *civitates*. The origin of Luther's doctrine would seem to be certified beyond all doubt as soon as we remember this Augustinian monk's own admission that he was an avid reader of Augustine. However, the genealogy is by no means this simple.[8]

The ultimate source of Luther's idea is undoubtedly to be found in the sublime conception of the spiritual father of Christian Europe who has always exerted a great influence on the best minds of the continent. But closer examination soon reveals the extent to which Luther deviated from Augustine. It is probably only of secondary importance to our study that each had a different conception of the basic nature of the State,[9] but it is a matter of primary importance that they deviated essentially in their views concerning the Christian's situation in the world.

According to Augustine, both cities are literally intermixed on earth, and the citizens of both will be separated only at the end of time. Meanwhile (literally, in the interval), it is possible to be a citizen of only one city and impossible to have a double passport. Luther also saw the two kingdoms against an eschato-

[7] Cf. J. Heckel, "Der Ansatz einer evangelischen Sozialethik bei M. Luther," in *Die Kirche in der Welt* (Munich, 1957), pp. 49-67; more recently, J. Heckel, "Das blinde, undeutliche Wort 'Kirche,'" in *Gesammelte Aufsätze* (Cologne, 1964), pp. 266-87. The counterpart of this "juridical" interpretation is D. Bonhoeffer's "dialectical" exegesis of Luther in *Nachfolge* (Munich, [7]1961), pp. 238-41 ("Die sichtbare Gemeinde").

[8] Cf. E. Kinder, "Gottesreich und Weltreich bei Augustin und bei Luther," in *Gedenkschrift für W. Elert* (Berlin, 1955), pp. 24-42.

[9] Cf. H. Arquillière, *L'augustinisme politique. Essai sur la formation des théories politiques au moyen âge* (Paris, [2]1954) and the earlier but still quite fundamental work of H. Scholz, *Glaube und Unglaube in der Weltgeschichte. Ein Kommentar zu Augustins De civitate Dei* (Leipzig, 1911), pp. 99-133.

logical background and maintained that here and now they could not be distinguished socially. But for Luther, the Christian was in the interim a citizen of two worlds, in accordance with God's will. This meant that he was constantly faced with an ethical dilemma. He was always asking himself: "What am I to do? Must I live in this situation as a member of the spiritual kingdom, or does God wish me to appear as a member of the worldly kingdom? Am I, here and now, a *persona privata* or a *persona publica*? Must I suffer and endure in the spirit of the Sermon on the Mount, or must I exercise order, discipline and compulsion for the sake of others?"

The struggle between the two cities, which for Augustine was always, so to speak, an immense social conflict, was for Luther an individual Christian problem, because the Christian was a citizen of both kingdoms.[10] Augustine saw the City of God on pilgrimage *hic in terra* using but not enjoying, satisfied but not fulfilled, restless but tranquil, in the knowledge that this was simply his situation. Luther, on the other hand, always placed everything that belongs *hic in terra* in the worldly kingdom and thereby preserved a purely spiritual *regnum* where Christ really ruled.

Various interpretations of the Augustinian idea were current in the medieval Church, and these often deviated widely from Augustine's original thought, both in their questionable shift of emphasis from the spiritual to the temporal sphere and in their too facile application of his idea to empirical factors such as Church and State.[11] Christianity on pilgrimage was frequently seen as inhabiting its temporal house as a home. Many modern authors are of the opinion that Luther's sharp division marked an essential breakthrough in the medieval system and brought an end to the confused intermixture.[12] According to these writers,

[10] This distinction, which in my opinion is fundamental, is neglected in Bornkamm's otherwise excellent analysis, *op. cit.,* footnote 3, pp. 37-43.

[11] E. Gilson, *Les métamorphoses de la Cité de Dieu* (Louvain, 1952).

[12] For example, Bornkamm, *op. cit.,* footnote 3, p. 33; Schuurman, *op. cit.,* footnote 1, pp. 241-3, 251; G. de Ruggiero, *Rinascimento, Riforma e Contrariforma (Storia della filosofia,* III) (Bari, ⁷1964), p. 219.

his sharp criticism of *perversio* (the wrongful confusion of the spiritual and the secular: he accused papists and other adversaries above all of making this transposition[13] and his protest against *confusio* was the deathblow to the medieval relationship between the Church and the world. In Bornkamm's view, Luther saw through and analyzed the ideology of the Middle Ages and made it disappear.[14]

Then come the questions: How is this possible? Or rather, how was this possible for him? Was Martin Luther really clever enough to see through his own period so clearly? Did he really intend to assault the ecclesiastical and social pattern of his own time? Did this man, who was basically so conservative, so averse to everything that savored of revolution and radical change,[15] really develop his doctrine of the two kingdoms for this purpose? The answer is by no means easy, for we are so readily swayed by sympathy for, or antipathy to, Luther or the Middle Ages. For the time being, one negative answer must suffice. Augustine cannot help us in our search for the origin of Luther's doctrine, for it is too much of an illegitimate child, and Augustine is only in appearance its spiritual father.

LUTHER'S ORIGINALITY?

Our question about the origin of the doctrine directs our attention toward the young Luther. Anyone who takes the trouble to arrange the numerous texts on the two kingdoms in chronological order will soon discover that clear textual material is only available from 1520 onward. A search for the possible existence of allusions to the two kingdoms before this date may therefore throw some light on its origin.

In August, 1518, Luther published his *Resolutiones disputa-*

[13] "Er [i.e., the Pope] hat es umbkehret und ist nu mit seiner geistlichen oberkait gar zu einer weltlichen oberkait worden" (*Weimar-Ausg.* 10, I, 2, p. 245). "Schwermer mengen ynn einander weltlich und christlich regiment" (*Weimar-Ausg.* 34, I, p. 122). Cf. footnote 6.

[14] Bornkamm, *op. cit.,* footnote 3, pp. 33, 42.

[15] "Profondément antidémocrate": E. Léonard, *Histoire générale du Protestantisme,* I (Paris, 1961), p. 76.

tionum de indulgentiarum virtute, submitted to Pope Leo X and written in defense of his theses on indulgences that had in the meantime become notorious.[16] At the end of his treatise, Luther asked whether theologians who go counter to Rome ought not to fear the double sword wielded by the Roman Church. Then he declaimed: "I should like to know who invented that commentary [on Luke 22, 38] attributing both a spiritual and a material sword to the pope! It is a commentary of the devil! The apostle [in Eph. 6, 17] was speaking only of the sword of God's Word. . . ."[17] This text, which quite clearly expresses opposition to the abuse of spiritual power for purely temporal measures of coercion (the typical *confusio*), is sometimes regarded as the first clear break with fundamentally medieval views. Certainly this notorious *"gladii* text" has for centuries been very popular with theologians, canonists and political theorists in their arguments about the double *auctoritas,* about spiritual and temporal power, and about the pope and the emperor or the bishop and the king—the medieval interpretations are as numerous as modern explanations! [18]

For the purpose of our inquiry, however, the only important question is whether this text indicates a break with a medieval system and its replacement by a new conception of the relationship between the spiritual and the worldly spheres. The answer is clear: Luther's tirade against this traditional gloss had itself been traditional for two centuries. Repeated and copied again and again from the *Decretum Gratiani* with characteristically medieval faithfulness to traditional material, this text had been just as faithfully contested from the time that Ockham and Marsilius of Padua had critically questioned an untenable exegesis.[19]

[16] *Weimar-Ausg.,* I, pp. 525-628 (ed. *Clemen,* ⁵I, pp. 15-147).

[17] *Weimar-Ausg.,* I, p. 624 (ed. *Clemen,* ⁵I, pp. 141-2).

[18] A recent bibliographical review of medieval political theories was provided by A. Weiler, "Church Authority and Government in the Middle Ages," in *Concilium 7: Historical Problems of Church Renewal* (1965), pp. 123-36. For the *gladii* text, see the well-known studies of A. Stickler and several examples in M. Wilks, "The Problem of Sovereignty in the Later Middle Ages," in *Cambridge Studies in Medieval Life and Thought,* New Series 9 (Cambridge, 1963), pp. 261-71, 308-9.

[19] G. de Lagarde, *La naissance de l'esprit laïque au déclin du moyen âge,* IV (Louvain, 1962), pp. 181-3; V (Louvain, 1963), p. 336.

Both legalists and canonists had rejected any appeal to this text of Luke as pure allegory without any conclusive force; they had other grounds for their dualism or papalism. This passage, then, provides no new evidence, since Luther was simply repeating what he might have read in Ockham and what had been repeated by John of Paris, Marsilius of Padua, Achellini and, in his own time, J. Almain and Latomus.[20]

However, very little attention has been given to Luther's exegesis of the *Our Father* in this context, and this seems far more promising. The second petition, *adveniat regnum tuum,* offered excellent opportunities to someone who wished to distinguish the spiritual and the worldly kingdoms and who saw, in the confusion of both, the prevailing sin of his own time. If the various versions of Luther's commentary on the *Our Father* are placed side by side, the following exegesis is obtained. "Thy kingdom is grace and virtue; here below all is sin and evil. Christ is Lord in thy kingdom; the evil one is the leader of the other kingdom. In this second petition, we ask thee to keep all sin from the one kingdom and to promote all the virtues of thy kingdom in us." [21] Clearly, what we have here is a preacher using the antithesis of good and evil to construct a moral example about virtues and vices.

This simple application is all the more striking when we examine Gabriel Biel's commentary on the same text in his *Expositio super canonem Missae* and remember that Luther had read this with emotion shortly before writing his own commentary. What Biel says is this: "The kingdom of grace rules in the hearts of the faithful; the devil's kingdom is the opposite. We pray that the sinners from the devil's kingdom may become citizens of thy kingdom. In this way, the community of the elect must grow as long as it continues to live here intermixed with the community of

---

[20] H. de Lubac, *Exégèse médiévale* (Théologie, 59), IV (Paris, 1964), pp. 381-4.

[21] Summarized from fragments of a sermon given at Wittenberg in 1516 (*Weimar-Ausg.,* 1, pp. 89-94), the "Auslegung für die einfaltigen Laien" (*Weimar-Ausg.,* 2) and the "Kurze Form" and the "Auslegung" (*Weimar Ausg.,* 6), all from 1519, and from "Eine kurze Form" of 1520 (*Weimar Ausg.,* 7), ed. *Clemen,* ⁵II, p. 54.

the evil ones, with Babylon, the *civitas confusionis*".[22] There is a clear echo of Augustine here which is much more striking than in the case of Luther and completely in accordance with medieval exegesis.

It is possible to use texts of this kind as valid evidence of the beginning of a new doctrine of the two kingdoms only if they are seen exclusively in the light of the writer's later development. Seen against the normal medieval background of theological and canonical writing of the period, they are in no way remarkable and cannot be regarded as important in our argument.

THE DECISIVE SPIRITUALIZATION

The situation, however, began to change in 1520. The contrasts became sharper after the Imperial Diet of Augsburg in 1518 and the Leipzig disputation of 1519. Luther knew that a denunciation was being prepared in Rome and that Germany had its eye on him. It was the year of the bull of excommunication and of the three famous treatises, *An den christlichen Adel* (June), *De captivitate Babylonica* (October) and the splendid *Von der Freiheit eines Christenmenschen* (November). The first two in particular reveal the doctrine of the *regna* in its essential elements,[23] but a treatise that is less well known than the three classic writings of the Reformation seems more important in connection with our investigation. This is the book *Von dem Papsttum zu Rom*, which was published in June of the same year.[24]

This vigorous defense was written in reaction to the argument

---

[22] J. Heckel, *op. cit.*, footnote 7, pp. 276-8, in which the author draws attention to this parallel. What is remarkable is that Luther, who had read this, did not make any commentary on this place; see H. Degering, *Randbemerkungen zu G. Biels Collectorium und Super canonem Missae* (Weimar, 1933). Cf. also H. Oberman, *The Harvest of Medieval Theology. G. Biel and Late Medieval Nominalism* (Cambridge, Mass., 1963), pp. 419-22 (*Corpus Christianum*).

[23] In Schuurman, *op. cit.*, footnote 1, there are twenty-one quotations from these alone.

[24] *Weimar-Ausg.*, 6, pp. 285-324 (ed. *Clemen*, [5]I, pp. 323-61).

put forward by A. von Alfeld of Leipzig University in his *Super apostolica Sede*. In this treatise, Alfeld maintained, among other things, that the Old Testament was fulfilled in the papacy, that the ancient priesthood was corporal and external and prefigured what was now spiritually fulfilled in the high priesthood of the Apostolic See. (This, of course, is a typical example of late medieval exegesis, which frequently saw the literal and corporal fulfillment of the Old Testament texts in contemporary ecclesiastical situations.) Luther's protest "against the renowned Romanist of Leipzig" (*wider den hochberühmten Romanisten zu Leipzig*) was: "Of course Aaron's priesthood is only external, since the spiritual, inward priesthood came only with Christ." [25] Apart from his other arguments, it was Alfeld's exegetical reasoning especially which impelled Luther to make his strenuous denial: "You, learned sir, assail God's Word with your intellect. You do not even listen to what God is saying! You reason about a community with a head, but what nonsense—that is reasoning based on temporal considerations. I must make it clear to your coarse brain what Christianity is. Scripture speaks clearly of one Christianity, as of a spiritual unity. Everything external and called spiritual (office, liturgy, etc.) is unbiblical and forms a corporal, external Christianity as opposed to the real, single, inward Christianity with which it is shamefully confused. Show me where your opinion can be found in the bible! Your reasoning is natural and you apply categories that are human and worldly to the Church or Christianity. That is against God's Word, which teaches us about spiritual matters only. . . ." [26]

This marks a decisive step forward in Luther's writings: the spiritual and the worldly are placed side by side with, and opposite to, each other in a way that is quite unmedieval and unlike Augustine. It is precisely because Luther does this so cautiously (even warning against division!) that it is so interesting historically, providing us, as it does, with an example of a first attempt in this direction.

[25] Schuurman, *op. cit.*, footnote 1, pp. 149-51.
[26] *Weimar-Ausg.*, 6, pp. 290-7 (ed. *Clemen*, ⁵I, pp. 329-36).

What, then, has happened here? Luther was attacking an
exegete whose aim was to establish proof of the historically developed power of the papacy with biblical texts. Alfeld's treatise
was simply one of very many, and would seem to be no worse
than the others. Luther objected strongly to this fortuitous example of canonical or juridical exegesis. This misuse of scripture,
in the tense situation of mid-1520, made him aware of a discovery
that was perhaps as decisive as his experience "in the Tower" for
his view of justification: the spiritualization of the concept of the
Church and the ruthless interiorization of everything that was
meant by Christian life. Luther's treatise does not provide us with
any clear exposition of the two kingdoms, and the second—the
worldly kingdom—is scarcely defined at all in it. But, even at
this early, still undeveloped stage, it is possible to detect the beginning of a system of thought which matured quickly in Luther's
mind from 1520 onward and which was fully developed by 1523.

In this early writing, then, we have the nucleus of his doctrine
of the *regna,* his concern for a spiritual kingdom and his anxiety
for an inward Christianity.[27] Everything that he said later about
the worldly kingdom seems to have been formulated in the context of its antithesis to this spiritual kingdom. His attitude was
basically defensive, with the result that his many positive statements about secular authority and about the position, status and
work of the Christian in the world are all fundamentally negative.
Ultimately, what they all come to is: Do not touch the spiritual
kingdom! For Luther, it was the very inviolability of this spiritual
kingdom which made the worldly kingdom so massive. Everything that belonged *hic in terra* was placed in the category of the
worldly kingdom, so that all that was left was Christ's pure kingdom.[28]

[27] Cf. Y. Congar, *Vraie et fauuse réforme* (Paris, 1950), pp. 425-7.

[28] There is therefore no reference to "evangelization" of the world or
"christianization" of society; see W. Kooiman, *Luther, Cultuurgeschiedenis
van het Christendom* (Amsterdam, ²1957), pp. 1104-31, esp. p. 1108.
The author has drawn my attention to the fact that Luther's apparently
radical opposition, which in this study is seen as a consequence of Luther's
spiritualization, should be linked with the concept of *caritas,* which is
active in both *regna,* although *diverso modo.* This is a difficult problem,
perhaps more difficult for Christians today than for Luther himself.

But every time that we ask ourselves the question as to how he reached this point, we cannot help being struck by the fact that the problems under discussion in the texts quoted are always exegetical ones, and also by the fact that Luther is constantly accusing those whom he is attacking of reading more into the bible than the bible actually says. Luther's denial of his own theological training reached its culmination in his belief that scripture was not really known and that it was abused in order to canonize human systems and institutions. Schuurman has demonstrated clearly the extent to which Luther's repudiation of all *confusio* and his opposition to the abuse of the spiritual determined and formed his doctrine of the two kingdoms.[29] Schuurman's findings are also remarkably in accordance with those of de Lubac who, in a recent study, concluded that it was Luther's rejection of the misuse of exegesis that impelled him to continue further along the path that he had been following.[30]

Should a *solo* not be added to the already widely discussed "three *solas*"? What Luther was really doing in his doctrine of the two kingdoms was pleading the cause of one *solo regno,* i.e., *spirituali*. This *solo* shared the same tragic fate as the three classic *solas;* here, too, a just and necessary corrective became a one-sided emphasis. Originating as criticism of a basically traditional kind, it became, in a situation of conflict, a system. What Luther wrote shortly afterward—in *Von den christlichen Adel,* for example, about the abolition of the spiritual order—was only a consistent reference to an external and institutional worldly kingdom. Even his inconsistencies with regard to secular authority were inspired not only by the need for an appeal to the strong arm and by the conservative attitude of a man who was basically unpolitical, but above all by his concern for Christ's inviolable, untouchable, non-human and non-worldly kingdom.

If these incomplete notes merit any conclusion, it is this: Scandal caused by the medieval externalization of an Augustinian ideal was, to begin with, less revolutionary in Luther's case than it was, for example, in the case of Huss, Wyclif or Ockham. It

[29] Schuurman, *op. cit.,* footnote 1, *passim.*
[30] H. de Lubac, *op. cit.,* footnote 20, pp. 383-4.

was only when the conflict had broken out that this spiritualizing tendency developed in him. Beginning with an appeal to scripture, this tendency grew with a grandiose one-sidedness that was inspired by religious zeal until it impelled him to the extreme step of separating what should have been distinguished for the sake of the one, spiritual, Christian kingdom.

After the event, it is possible for us to see Luther's doctrine of the two kingdoms as his struggle with a confused medieval view of the world. The whole of that motley late medieval world in its religious poverty undoubtedly crept into the theory of the worldly kingdom; but that, of course, is a different subject.

Both the Catholic Church and the Churches of the Reformation have been actively concerned with this problem from Luther's time up to the present day. Perhaps—this is not simply another subject, or even a question of Church history—they may from now on be able to discover together that both the medieval system and the doctrine of the two kingdoms belong to the past history of a Church which, made wise by the bitter experience of both, will once more begin to reflect not on her *regnum,* but on her *servitium in mundo.*

Jean Leclercq, O.S.B. / *Clervaux, Luxembourg*

The Bible and the Gregorian Reform

I
t is difficult to discuss the bible in the Middle Ages—a period that lasted for a thousand years.[1] I therefore propose to limit my discussion to the reform which has come to be known as the "Gregorian Reform", named after Pope Gregory VII. Although the reform in question had begun before Gregory VII, it gained intensity under his influence, when under the name of Hildebrand he held the office of Archdeacon of the Church of Rome, and it continued after his death. It was, therefore, both long and complex, and an exhaustive treatment of it here would not be feasible, especially since the part played in it by the bible has hardly been examined at all. Out of the mass of work relating to the subject, only one title deals with this theme: Hackelsperger's *The Bible and the Idea of Empire in the Middle Ages: A Contribution to the Study of the Use of the Bible in the Dispute between the Empire and the Papacy in the Time of the Salian Franks*,[2] a conscientious work, the title and subtitle of which indicate that it is concerned only with one aspect of the problem: the use of the bible in political controversies. However, the Gregorian Reform covered a number of areas other than that of religious politics; historians today are more severe than in the

---

[1] Cf. H. De Lubac, *Exégèse médiévale* (4 vols.) (Paris, 1959-1966).

[2] Hackelsperger, *Bibel und mittelalterlicher Reichsgedanke. Studie und Beiträge zum Gebrauch der Bibel im Streit zwischen Kaiser und Papsttum zur Zeit der Salier* (Bottrop-in-Westfalien, 1934).

past with the latter, while investigation of the former has scarcely begun.

The word to define in *The Bible and Reform in the Middle Ages* is "reform". What does it mean? Gerhart Ladner has recently provided a precise and valuable investigation in his book, *The Idea of Reform: Its Impact on Christian Thought and Action in the Age of the Fathers.*[3] He examines the biblical idea expressed by *reformare–reformatio,* as well as the entire related vocabulary: *regenerare, renasci, renovare, reparare, restaurare, restituere, resurgere,* etc.; then he traces the evolution of the idea though the patristic period. One point to be made here is that the idea of *reformatio* is associated with *renovatio* in the letter to the Romans: *Nolite conformari huic saeculo, sed reformamini in novitate sensus vestri* ("And you must not fall in with the manners of this world; there must be an inward change, a remaking of your minds. . . .").[4]

Ladner has clearly shown that, for the Fathers of the Church, reform is, above all, this "remaking" of the Christian and not of the Church and its juridical and disciplinary structures; its end is the constant restoration of the image of God in man. But in the Middle Ages, and particularly in the 11th century, that idea seems to have assumed the meaning of a reform of the Church and society. If so, one might ask whether the change was made at the price of a limitation and impoverishment of the biblical notion of reform, whether the notion contained in scripture had been twisted into a meaning foreign to it. These questions must be answered by the testimony of facts. The investigation should bear on two distinct but complementary aspects: the reform of persons, which we shall call the interior reform, and the reform of institutions, the exterior reform. Therefore, we shall examine successively the reforms that Ladner termed "individual" and "supra-individual": in other words, the reform of Christians and the

[3] G. Ladner, *The Idea of Reform. Its Impact on Christian Thought and Action in the Age of the Fathers* (Harvard University Press, 1959).
[4] Rom. 12, 2. In this text, *metamorphoūsde,* translated by *reformamini* in the Vulgate (Vg) and in D (old European text), is rendered by *transformemini* in the version quoted by St. Cyprian (K).

reform of Christianity.[5] The facts themselves will point to certain conclusions on the role of the bible in the Gregorian Reform.

I

THE REFORM OF CHRISTIANS

It should be observed immediately that in the 11th and 12th centuries the biblical vocabulary dealing with the idea of *reformatio* was rarely applied to the Church as a whole: it continued to be used exclusively with reference to the interior renewal of the Christian.[6] This reform of every Christian and of all Christians was realized within the framework of groups of Christians which, for the sake of clarity, we shall consider successively: clergy, monks and laity.

(a) *The Clergy*

Obviously, reform of the clergy is concerned with reform of the laity, for whom they are preeminently responsible. Its goal is to lead the clergy to live more in accordance with the scriptures, the better to teach the scriptures to the faithful. Hence the insistence of Gregory VII and his collaborators on a return to the "makeup of the primitive Church", to the "one heart and one soul" of the original apostolic community;[7] hence their emphasis on the advantages of the common life and on the demands of

[5] The word *Christianitas* was then sometimes used as equivalent to *populus Christianus* and *Christiana plebs*. For a bibliography on this subject, cf. G. Ladner, *op. cit.*, p. 424, and Y. Congar, "L'Eglise chez S. Anselme," in *Spicilegium Beccense* I (Paris, 1957), p. 393, n. 111.

[6] The word *reformare* is often found applied to peace (*reformare pacem*) and sometimes to a rite or monastery or even a particular Church; it then usually has the non-biblical sense of "giving back", "restoring to" or making good an injury by means of repayment. However, it is not used —or at least I have found no text in which it is—in the sense of *reformatio Ecclesiae*, so widely discussed in the 15th century at the time of the conciliar crisis and thereafter. On the other hand, "interior reform" and the "restoration of the original image of God" were still talked of. This simple fact of terminology indicates that interior reform was not lost sight of, but was rather maintained by fidelity to the language and doctrine of St. Paul.

[7] Cf. G. Ladner, *op. cit.*, pp. 384, 402.

evangelical poverty. Gregory VII would base his entire pastoral ministry on "the pages of the prophets and the gospels";[8] he states that, in the choice of a bishop, "the first concern must be his conformity to the authority of the Gospel and canon law".[9]

The polemics on the mores of the clergy are filled with scriptural arguments—one might almost say they are cluttered with them. The sin of simony—receiving or administering the sacraments for money—received its name from Simon the Magician (Acts of the Apostles),[10] who himself had been preceded by Balaam, Gehazi, Jason (2 Macc. 4, 7) and Judas Iscariot, and all the biblical texts condemning avarice are quoted in denunciation of the practice.[11] Likewise, incontinent members of the clergy were termed "Nicolaitans", after the *Nicolaitae* of the Apocalypse.[12]

This text and others draw attention to another aspect of the Gregorian Reform, to which historians, preoccupied almost exclusively with political situations, tend to pay little consideration. We shall return later to the value of these appeals to scripture, but it is necessary at this point to establish their existence, as they presuppose a regular study of the whole bible, aiming to spread this among the clergy and, through them, the laity. One of the primary objectives of the Gregorian Reform was to promote a renewal of the pastoral ministry, the *cura animarum,* both the condition and the result of which would be a more widespread knowledge of the Word of God.

(b) The Monks

On the subject of the monastic reforms of the 11th and 12th centuries, which together constitute what may be considered a vast renewal of monasticism, much might well be said; indeed, much remains to be studied. The bible is as much an element in

[8] Cf. E. Caspar (ed.), Gregorii VII registrum IV, 281, *Mon. Germ. Hist., Epistolae selectae* (Berlin, 1955), p. 344.

[9] *Ibid.,* V. p. 353.

[10] On this point I have presented texts in "Simoniaca haeresis," in *Studi Gregoriani* I (Rome, 1947), pp. 523-30.

[11] Cf. Hackelsperger, *op. cit.,* pp. 100-8.

[12] Apoc. 21 and 16.

the writings of the monastic reformers as in the case of the clerical reform. It is deemed more important than the Desert Fathers or the witnesses of early monasticism. By the 10th century, St. Odo, second Abbot of Cluny, had already set out his program of reform in a sweeping poem of biblical inspiration called *Occupatio*.[13] However, the use of the bible here implies a selection; the monks were looking for particular themes in the bible, and even for an overall view of Christianity. These themes inspired them more intensely than others, as witness the intensity of their portrayal in works of art such as the capitals of the cloister at Moissac.[14]

Although the bible was used to promote a renewal of the institution of monasticism, it was also, and to an even greater extent, used as a means of interior renewal of the monks themselves. By the 12th century, this movement had produced a profoundly biblical literature, such as that of St. Bernard whose works on the reform of institutions—monasteries, bishoprics and the Roman Curia—were all grounded on a theology of the restoration of the image of God in man.[15]

(c) *The Laity*

The pastoral activity of the clergy and the influence of the monasteries also reached the laity. In a number of monasteries, commentaries on scripture were given to the people, at least under certain circumstances. In several places, the liturgical drama enacted biblical scenes. Some recent studies have demonstrated the influence of early translations of the bible into Romance and Germanic languages in novels and other literary works of the time.[16]

[13] A. Swobada, ed. (Leipzig, 1900).

[14] These capitals have been studied by J. Hourlier in "La spiritualité à Moissac d'après la sculpture," in *Moissac et l'Occident au XIe siècle* (Toulouse, 1964), pp. 71-80.

[15] The word *reformatio* is used in a Pauline context by St. Bernard in *De diversis, Serm. II* (*Patr. Lat.* 183, 545A) and in *Sup. Cant.*, 74, 6, ed. *S. Bernardi opera* II (Rome, 1958), 243, 24. *Reformare* is frequent in the Pauline sense indicated by the context; cf., for example, *Sup. Cant.*, 14, 5, ed. *S. Bernardi opera* I (Rome, 1957), 79, 13.

[16] Cf. the works indicated in *Cahiers de civilisation médiévale* VII (1964), bibliography of nn. 749, 1010, 1184 and 1788.

The manner of presenting the bible had long varied in different circumstances. As a result, though the people were able to have some acquaintance with the bible, a true biblical culture remained a clerical monopoly. However, from the 11th century onward, the laity began to grow aware of itself, encouraged by every pastoral effort toward reform. The people also began to look to the bible for support. Popular religious movements and itinerant preachers derived great success from appealing to the authority of the Gospel. They, too, were tempted to pick and choose from the immense arsenal of the scriptures, and their choices, by excluding certain ideas or concentrating excessively on others, gave rise to abuses. As we have seen, the clergy and its leaders found in the sacred books arguments that supported the causes they served, which could have brought into being a sort of "clerical bible" (or at least a clerical use of the bible), just as, as we shall see, a "political bible" existed at the same time. A "lay", even "anti-clerical", bible also appeared. A specialist on the subject has described the evangelism of the Church of the Gospel and the ideal of the popular piety of the time, in these words:

"The Church of the *Vita Apostolica* is an open Church, in continuity with Judaism, welcoming every man of goodwill, and apparently imposing no condition on his entry into the community of the faithful. The Church of the Gospel, as seen by the masses, is a Church of the good, as opposed to the Church of the wicked; it is often a Church of the poor, as opposed to the Church of the rich, a Church with a defensive character, a citadel against outsiders and, above all, against heretics. . . .

"The Gospel, as it is believed and lived, is not the Gospel in its entirety, such as the one studied by the clergy. It does not usually bring in St. John—who was discovered only at the end of the Middle Ages as a result of an interiorization of religious sentiment—or the dogmatic passages of the Synoptics; it is essentially the Gospel according to St. Matthew. . . . It is the Gospel of 'Christ according to the flesh', more ethical than dogmatic, leaving place for resentment, as though Luke's text on the Beatitudes is preferable to that of Matthew: resentment against monks, against bad priests, against the rich and the powerful, resentment in which it is often difficult to distinguish between anger and a frustrated sense of justice and brotherhood." [17]

Therefore, "a popular Church, spontaneous, instinctive, more attached to the Gospel than to canon law",[18] tended to appear in opposition to the hierarchical Church. The leaders of the Gregorian Reform were aware of the danger, and they tried to eliminate it by means of a better understanding of scripture among the clergy and, through them, the laity. At least the eagerness of the people to have scripture quoted to them explains the immense part the bible played in the polemics aroused by the reform of institutions.

II

THE REFORM OF CHRISTENDOM

From one of its aspects—that which left the most noticeable mark on literary sources and which has consequently most occupied historical research—the Gregorian Reform appears as a struggle for influence between the papacy and the princes, particularly between Pope Gregory VII and Emperor Henry IV. The Roman Pontiff claimed a greater liberty of action in the government and reform of the universal Church and in that of particular Churches. When his claims were challenged, he both had to justify and to affirm the supremacy of his power. The long and difficult quarrel that ensued produced much in writing from both parties. Our task will be to examine the place given therein to the bible.

All those involved invoked the bible. Hackelsperger has placed at the end of his thesis on *The Bible and the Idea of Empire* an index of the scriptural references he noted in the polemical literature of the period. A partial collection of this literature appears in the three volumes of *Monumenta Germaniae Historiae* under the title of *Libelli de Lite Imperatorum et Pontificum, Saeculi*

---

[17] E. Delaruelle, "La vie commune des clercs et la spiritualité populaire au XI siècle," in *La vita commune* . . . I, p. 172.
[18] *Ibid.*, p. 173.

XI et XII, in which about a hundred writings fill more than two thousand large pages, although all is not included. There are quoted more than seven hundred passages from the bible, roughly as many from the Old Testament as from the New. From the Old Testament, the Pentateuch, the historical books (in particular, the Books of Kings) and the prophets are most often quoted; in the New Testament, the gospels and the letters of St. Paul provide the greatest number of texts.[19]

These figures are eloquent but insufficient. In a study on *The Scriptural Sources of the Thought of Gregory VII,* Arquillère examined the influence of the Old Testament, and subsequently the contribution—decisive, as we have seen—of the New Testament toward *the spirit of love, the spirit of faith* and *the idea of justice.*[20] It remains for future research to further the investigation, to extend it to the works of other authors and to evaluate the results. We must be satisfied here with a few indications.

When justifying papal power, Gregory VII and his supporters appeal to Gospel texts which speak of the role entrusted to Peter, such as "Feed my lambs",[22] "Lend strength to your brothers",[23] "You are Peter, and upon this rock",[24] and so forth. Similarly, in the Roman curia, a verse from Jeremiah was applied to the universal pastoral responsibility of the Roman pontiff: "Behold, I have set you over nations and over kingdoms." [25] However, this verse was invoked "in a context of correction and reform, a context of abuse to uproot and disorder to resolve, much as St. Bernard was later to do".[26] Only later, particularly from the time of Boniface VIII, was this verse used as a clear expression of pontifical authority. On the other hand, in Gregory's own time, the verse from the first letter to the Corinthians: "A man gifted with

---

[19] Cf. Hackelsperger, *op. cit.,* pp. 130-6: Register der Bibelstellen.
[20] *Saint Gregoire VII* (Paris, 1934), pp. 222-72.
[22] John 21, 15.
[23] Luke 22, 31-32.
[24] Matt. 16, 18. Cf. G. Miccoli, "Le ordinazioni simoniache nel pensiero di Gregorio VII," in *Studi medievali* IV, 1 (1963), p. 116, pointing out the frequency with which these texts were quoted by Gregory VII.
[25] Jer. 1, 10.
[26] Y. Congar, "Ecce constitui te super gentes (Jer. 1, 10)," in *Theologie in Geschichte und Gegenwart* (Melanges M. Schmaus) (ed. J. Auer-H. Volk) (Munich, 1957), p. 679.

the Spirit can judge the worth of everything, but is not himself subject to judgment by his fellowmen",[27] was used as an argument in favor of the adage *Prima sedes a nemine iudicatur*.[28] Perhaps, as has been suggested [29] in translating *anakrinein* by *iudicare*, which does not render the exact nuance, the Vulgate inclined interpretation toward a judicial order, rather than a "spiritual" one, in the Pauline sense of the word.[30] It is perhaps, above all, St. Paul's term *spiritualis* (*pneumatikos*) which has undergone a change in meaning from the charismatic capacity to discern and judge—a capacity proceeding from the fact that man is one with Christ[31]—to a juridical and official power. In these matters as in others, one must appreciate the merits and shortcomings, the richness and the deficiency of the Vulgate and other Latin translations.[32] However, until the time of Gregory VII, this text retained its moral import. New circumstances were required to make people think of changing the meaning to that of a juridical power. This occurred at the same time when others, also trained in the Christian disciplines, were using the Gospel and the Pauline texts that limited the judiciary power of the pope in support of the opposite proposition. According to them, Christ himself had admitted being judged when he said: "If I spoke amiss, state it in evidence. . . ." [33] Nor were the words of St. Paul in his letter to the Galatians forgotten: "I opposed him [Peter] to his face." [34]

[27] 1 Cor. 2, 15.

[28] On this point, Fr. Congar was kind enough to send me the manuscript of an unpublished study, and I wish here to acknowledge my debt to him.

[29] A. Koeniger, "Prima sedes a nemine iudicatur," in *Beiträge, zur Geschichte des christlichen Alterums und der Byzantinischen Literatur* (Festgabe A. Ehrland) (Bonn, 1922), pp. 280-1.

[30] *Anakrínō* usually had a juridical sense in Greek literature and in the Septuagint, meaning the judicial inquiry which led to the trial and sentence. Cf. the excellent article by Buschel in G. Kittel, *Theologisches Worterbuch zum Neuen Testament,* III (Stuttgart, 1938), pp. 945-6.

[31] This springs from the context, particularly the following verse (16).

[32] Cf. *Richesses et déficiences des anciens psautiers latins* (Rome: Abbaye Saint-Jérôme, 1959).

[33] John 18, 33.

[34] Gal. 2, 11. Cf. Hackelsperger, *op. cit.,* p. 24. The authority attributed to St. Paul in the Gregorian texts has been studied by Y. Congar, "S. Paul et l'autorité de l'Eglise Romaine d'après la tradition," in *Studiorum paulinorum congressus internationalis catholicus, 1961* (Rome, 1963), pp. 504-6.

So evolved the battery of arguments for and against pontifical authority. John of Paris, at the end of the 13th century, was the first to attempt a synthesis, but it continued to contribute to contradictory apologetics over centuries of polemics, in fact almost up to the present.

This example should suffice to give some idea of the polemics involved. The centrality of the Law in the Old Testament was used to account for Roman centralization. Juridical consequences were drawn from such texts as those of St. Paul on the mystical body. The *fons aquae vitae* in Jeremiah[35] was interpreted as meaning that bishops received their jurisdiction from the pope. Texts from Leviticus on the exclusion of lepers were used to justify excommunication; recourse to the Old Testament was used to justify wars. The symbolism of the miter, throne, scepter, kissing of the feet, the ring and other insignia of the leaders and kings of Israel was applied to the pope and the bishops. In short, biblical themes, the meanings of which were hardly governmental, were turned into political arguments.[36] There was no question of a monopoly of the bible in this connection by the partisans of pontifical theocracy; as we have seen, their adversaries applied the same method, often even to the same texts. All sought in the bible support of the ideas of the times and culture or justification of the causes they wished to promote. Instead of objectively scrutinizing the bible, they interpreted it, used it and bent it to fit their own current needs. They took a number of texts out of context and applied them to their own particular concept of reform and of who was competent to carry out its reform. Consequently, in spite of the large quantity of biblical texts used, the significance of each was truncated and the fullness of the message of the whole bible was narrowed. Such are the facts that history forces us to admit. It remains, in conclusion, to indicate the problems those facts disclose.

---

[35] Jer. 2, 13.

[36] For the biblical applications just noted, texts are quoted in W. Ullmann, "The Bible and Principles of Government in the Middle Ages," in *La Bibbia nell' alto medioevo* (Spoleto, 1963), pp. 206-26.

CONCLUSION

The problems may be summarized in two principal questions, one historical, the other theological.

1. The first concerns the judgment one can pass on the Gregorian Reform: to determine whether it marked a break with the concept of reform, until then traditional in Christianity. We have seen that both the word "reform" and the idea have their origin in the teaching of St. Paul on the renovation of man by the Spirit of God: *Reformamini in novitate sensus vestri.* This text from the letter to the Romans has always been proclaimed in the Western liturgy in the Mass of the 1st Sunday after Epiphany; the Collect of the feast of the Epiphany uses the same vocabulary in the same sense: *intus reformari mereamur.* The idea, then, might appear to be that of an exclusively interior reform which would not reach the exterior, the externals of life, the institution or, in today's parlance, the structures of the Church. St. Augustine, whose influence in the West during the Middle Ages was so great that the expression "political Augustinianism" was coined, had taught that if each Christian must wage a battle within himself (the battle which furnished the theme of the book *De Agone Christiano*), if each Christian must struggle to reform and correct himself, if each Christian has to unite himself to others in order to improve society and the world, then charity obliges him to tend to the good of all, to the *vita socialis,* to a personal reform in common.[37] Far from there being an incompatibility between interior and exterior reform, the former demands the latter, tends to it, and is its condition and its beginning, its "principle" which the latter helps.

The Gregorian Reform did indeed conserve and realize this traditional concept of reform insofar as circumstances permitted. Gregory VII applied the Pauline vocabulary of personal reform to an institutional reform. Following the current which had originated long before them, he and those who worked with him for a renovation of the Church in their times felt that the Church

[37] Cf. G. Ladner, *The Idea of Reform,* pp. 402-24.

as a juridical organism had to develop, order, institutionalize and adapt the material contained in the Old and New Testaments to particular historical needs. In conciliar decrees and canonical works of the era, the bible was always a source of inspiration and it was often quoted. Western mentality inclined toward practical solutions rather than abstract concepts, and in order to find, formulate and gain acceptance for them, it turned to the Old Testament as an ideal, especially on the subject of religious society in relation to secular power, while the New Testament furnished the final solutions. In *Hibernensis,* a 7th-century collection of canon law, there are no less than five hundred passages from the bible, each of them preceded by the simple title *Lex.* Thus the Gregorian Reform maintained the union of the bible and canon law. Only in the following period were the two disciplines separated, when Gratian and Peter Lombard collected, each on his own side, the *auctoritates* that were to serve as basic texts for a long time.

Gregory VII and the Gregorians, many of them monks and all of them influenced by St. Augustine, conceived of reform as an essentially spiritual matter. For them, as for their master, there could be no reform of the Church without reform of the Christian. In both aspects of reform, the goal was not innovation, but renovation; it was not a question of destroying and rebuilding afterward, but of repairing, restoring and reforming what already existed. Reform therefore supposes a tradition, and tradition does not exist without the bible.

2. Here the second problem comes in: the value of the use of scripture by the Gregorian Reform. First of all, we must bear in mind that the bible was by no means absent from the reform; in fact, one might be tempted to say that its presence was excessive. There was no opposition to the bible for the simple reason that scripture offered arguments both for and against any proposition. One can say that the best minds made a more restrained and judicious use of scripture. For example, Gregory VII quoted the gospels more readily than the Old Testament on the subject of the reform of the Church. Father Congar has pointed out

that, on the subject of the relation of the two powers, the great
symbolic figures— Melchisedech, the sun and the moon, the two
swords, etc.—are lacking in St. Anselm, who "seems not to have
cultivated the art of allegory".

Moreover, we can distinguish the so-called medieval exegesis
—the use of the bible by theologians reflecting on the sources of
faith (the exegesis which Father de Lubac has primarily studied)
—from the use of holy scripture in polemics. In the latter, biblical
argumentation is superabundant in practically all the authors of
the time. This proves that a very real value was attributed to it.
In reading the hundred works conveniently collected in the three
volumes of the *Libelli de Lite,* we quickly become accustomed to
see the same texts used to support various theses, and we can
easily distinguish the value of one treatise from another. However, most of the readers of the Gregorian era had but few of
these texts before them, and they did not know those used by
their opponents. One can therefore understand the strong impression of any argumentation presented under the aegis of holy
scripture.

We have a very precise testimony to this. Honorius of Autun,
at the beginning of his treatise *Summa Gloria,* asks which of the
two powers is superior to the other, and declares that he could
easily answer in a few words. But he immediately adds: "To the
ignorant, however, or to those who are blinded by the wisdom
of the world, nothing is acceptable that is not confirmed by
numerous testimonies from the bible. We must therefore go back
to the beginning of the world." He then opens with his first
chapter on Adam as a figure of Christ, and continues on with
Abel, Cain, Nemroth ("Chief of the Tyrants") and fourteen
other chapters leading up to Christ. This text proves the impact
of the bible, particularly on the less learned; it also shows that
theologians who used scripture to satisfy the Christian people
knew well that all the arguments they borrowed from the bible
were not always conclusive, but that some of them served only
to illustrate and emphasize ideas which could be stated in another
way and more briefly. Biblical facts were used in chronological

order; it was not so much a sense of the history and the past experience of the People of God that was lacking, as a sense of evolution. The various phases of that past were seen as simultaneous, belonging to a present which had not undergone change and which continued even now in the Church. Their use of the bible was characterized by a too literal interpretation of the Old Testament, the texts of which were applied directly to historical situations in the Church, and by an insufficiently literal interpretation of certain passages of the New Testament. Indeed, there were certain excellent principles recalled, such as the following, inspired by St. John, which was formulated by a whole tradition going back to Tertullian and then passed through the declarations of Gregory VII, Urban II and Ivo of Chartres before entering the canonical works: "The Lord said, 'I am the way and the truth.' He did not say, 'I am the custom.' " Nevertheless, this and other equally valid ideas were applied out of context because the men who used them were unable to discern the exact meaning of other texts—a result of ignorance and the passionate conflicts aroused by opposing interests. These polemics unquestionably led to a narrowing of perspectives, a lessening of objectivity and an imposition of points of view and modes of interpretation that distorted the meaning of certain texts.

These facts underline by contrast the value of current progress in the biblical sciences and our discretion in the use of scripture today. However, what has changed since the Middle Ages is not the love and esteem of the bible, for, as we have seen, the Gregorian period was not lacking in these. What has changed is the understanding of the philological disciplines which help toward a more precise and accurate understanding of holy scripture.

In the Middle Ages there was a tendency to look to the bible as a source and justification for certain ideas and institutions which it did not in fact contain, and to seek in it solutions to problems which it never posed. Biblical discussion of the period therefore rested on partly invalid foundations. However, what can be accepted as valid is the conviction that reform—that *aggiornamento* which the texts of Vatican Council II call *accommodata renovatio*—is necessary, and that the reform of structures is conditioned by a reform of persons who renew themselves continually in the Spirit sent to the Church by Christ. A disinterested and objective study of the bible will greatly contribute to reform. The experience of the Middle Ages and particularly of the Gregorian Reform proves that interpretation and utilization of the Word of God must be separated from anything belonging to a particular culture or historical period that might limit its full meaning.

In this way we will be able to use those permanent and universal elements in the bible which are common to all Christians and capable of leading all men toward God.

Hilarion Petzold / *Neuss, Germany*

The Nature of Orthodoxy and the Medieval Serbian Church

lthough in *L'Eglise du Christ sur terre*[1] an attempt is made to give a valid definition of orthodoxy, no such definition can be said to possess binding authority. The decrees of the seven ecumenical councils offer no definition of the idea of the Church, nor is there any consensus on the subject among the Fathers. In fact, a definition does not seem possible, for "the nature of the Church is a mystery. This is . . . the basic feeling and conviction of every (Orthodox) Catholic. But there are two aspects to the mystery: on the one hand, it is a revelation, the opportunity to share in what is secret and holy, and, on the other, it is an experience of the absolute transcendence, the unknowability and boundlessness of that which infinitely surpasses any human capacity".[2] When the Fathers use a variety of images to describe the Church, such as the body of Christ, the new heavenly Jerusalem, the bride, the spiritual body, they are only replacing one idea with another of similar complexity. These images, however, do not define the Church in all its fullness, but simply suggest one particular aspect of it.

The theology of the Serbian Orthodox Church in the Middle Ages lays special emphasis on the following as criteria of the Church:

[1] S. Boulgakoff, *L'Orthodoxie* (Paris, [2]1958), p. 1.
[2] L. Zander, "Das geistig-religiöse Antlitz der Ostkirche," in *Das Christentum des Ostens und die christliche Einheit* (1965), p. 63.

I The love of God as it has been manifested in Christ.

II Eschatology and the consequent contempt for worldly goods.

III Cooperation with the State as the guardian of the divine order for the benefit of the Christian fold.

IV Theosis and community life on the basis of the conciliar, Orthodox faith.

I

THE LOVE OF GOD AS MANIFESTED IN CHRIST

According to the medieval Serbian documentary sources, the nature of the Orthodox Church is based on the deed that God performed through his Son. But since God is love (1 Jn. 4, 8.16), the reason for his action can only be love, and its effect can only be to bring forth love. In Christ and through Christ God himself has been active. He has taken an active part in history and thus altered both its contents and its direction. Here we catch sight of the supra-historical radiance of God's decision, his saving plan (*oikonomia*) to fill the whole universe with love. This is how we are to understand the old patristic saying: "Christ became man so that man might become God," i.e., in the terminology of medieval Serbian theology, ". . . so that man might become love." The basis of the Orthodox Church is this eternal love of God. God's love gives, irrespective of merit, and does good even when punishment is deserved. In the medieval Serbian sources,[3] of which we have used chiefly the writings of St. Sava (1169-1235) and the Old Serbian biographies of Serbian kings and saints, there are many references to God's love of man. A few characteristic examples will illustrate their point of view. Domentianus (Monastery of Hilandar), St. Sava's 13th-century biographer, says the following on this subject: "We men are not

[3] A considerable number of the source documents used for this essay were given to me by the Rev. Prof. D. Dimitrievió of the theological faculty of Belgrade University.

worthy of any attention; we are disobedient, we break God's commandments and anger him by our misdeeds. But in spite of this, God has not left us in our sins so that we would die in them, but he has come to us, shown us his goodness and cleansed our being from sin. That is what makes God's love so splendid, for it is not remarkable if the just man is saved, nor is it admirable if the pure man receives grace. In fact, grace is not grace if it is deserved." [4] In conversation, St. Sava said the following about the way God's love works in Christ: "Eternal and sacred love has been revealed to us. For our sake God has removed all evil from our minds through this love and purified our hearts. Out of this love he sent his Son into the world in order to draw through him the whole world to himself (Jn. 12, 32) and to save all who love him. God's love is so great that he did not spare even his beloved Son. He commanded him to die for all, so that we mortal men might also rise with him, see God in our flesh and know and feel his love. For everything in heaven and earth has been created by God out of love and is maintained by love. Through it God has invited us to him and given us true faith in his Son. If we know the Son and believe in him, then we shall understand the love of God, and that is the only love. For neither in heaven nor on earth is there any love that is outside the love of God. Truly, Christ is *God's love*. He will redeem all who love him and God and are just, for Jesus is just and pure and loves all men wonderfully." [5]

II

ESCHATOLOGY AND THE CONSEQUENT CONTEMPT FOR WORLDLY GOODS

The divine love of man is also the basis of the Church as the community of believers. Since the Church is not only a society, but essentially and primarily a community, for this reason alone

[4] Domentianus, *Životi Sv. Save i Sv. Simeona* (ed. L. Mirković) (Belgrade, 1938), pp. 124-5.
[5] *Ibid.*, pp. 143ff.

love must be one of its essential characteristics. Before all ages God founded the Church out of love as his act of salvation in Christ. Thus the Church is a community of love because it was founded out of love, because its members are united with one another in communal love, and because it is striving as a community for union with Christ, God's love. This striving, this orientation toward Christ, gives the life of the Church a heavenly, eschatological direction which is a central feature of the Orthodox Church of medieval Serbia and of the Orthodox Church as a whole.[6] There is an awareness of being only a wanderer, a stranger, a guest on earth, *in via*. Because of this the Church and its faithful direct all their yearning toward heaven in order "to be where Christ is (*in patria*) and to dwell with the saints in the kingdom of God".[7] The *Parousia* is longed for, and the second request of the Lord's Prayer, "Thy kingdom come", is one of the most important for the Orthodox Christian. Moreover, apocalyptic eschatological events are expected at the end of the world, and this idea especially dominates monastic life: "All prayers, singing, fasts, the many inclinations and all the mortifications are intended to dispose Christ to mercy at the Judgment." [8]

This expectation of, and orientation toward, the coming of Christ had an influence on all areas of Church life, and in the medieval Serbian Church it is impossible to make a distinction between the life of the Church and private life. The churches are built facing east, and the faithful pray facing east. The eucharistic gifts are raised by the priest toward the east. The faithful peasant ploughs his first furrow toward the east. The dead are buried facing east to await their Christ, "for as the lightning comes from the east . . . so will be the coming of the Son of Man" (Mt. 24, 27). Christ, "the light that knows no evening",[9] lights up in his *Parousia* the world and its goods,

[6] For the eschatology of the Eastern Church, cf. B. Stasiewski, "Die Überwindung der Geschichte durch die eschatalogische Grundhaltung der Ostkirche," in *Christentum und Geschichte* (Düsseldorf, 1955), p. 65.

[7] Sv. Sava, "Život svetog Simeona," in *Spisi svetog Save i Stevana Prvovencani* (ed. L. Mirković) (Belgrade, 1939), p. 135.

[8] Sv. Sava, "Hilandarski i studenički tipik," ch. 1, *op. cit.*, footnote 7.

[9] Byzantine liturgy.

so that their worth or worthlessness becomes apparent and all can see that he himself is true worth. "Worldly goods are transitory; they are quickly acquired and quickly lost. But the heavenly goods of Christ are eternal; they do not pass away and they are worth possessing. So, for the sake of Christ, one should renounce all worldly goods and use them rather (by bestowing gifts and alms) as a means to attaining heaven." [10] This eschatology of the Church also includes a personal expectation for the individual believer, a view which was strengthened in Serbia at the end of the Middle Ages by the invasion of the Turks and their reign of terror.

III

COOPERATION WITH THE STATE

This turning away from the world, which is by no means the same as alienation from reality, also determines the attitude of the medieval Serbian Church toward the State. Both the exercise of worldly power by the Church and the interference in the affairs of the Church by the State are incompatible with the nature of the Church, which is orientated toward the eternal and those events that will take place at the end of the world. Nevertheless, Church and State as independent bodies are to stand in a harmonious relationship with one another, since the order of the State also is rooted in the order of God. It is in these terms that the relation between the Serbian Church and the State is set out in the "Krmčija", the *Nomocanon* (Code of Canon Law) compiled by St. Sava from Byzantine sources.

The Krmčija contains neither the judgments of Homentianos and Balsamon, nor those of Ekloge in which the emperor is assigned papal power within the Church. Papal Caesarism is also condemned: "All bishops are equal, since they have all

---

[10] D. Dimitrijević, "Karakterne osobine etika s naročitim isticanjem sveto Savske etike," in *Zbornik Pravoslavnog bogoslovskog fakulteta*, II (Belgrade, 1951), pp. 288ff.

received divine grace in the same measure." St. Sava's Krmčija laid the foundation for the relationship between Church and State, and on this basis there arose in medieval Serbia an organic cooperation of these two institutions which is probably unique in history. An eloquent testimony to this harmonious relationship is the cultural flowering of the Serbian Middle Ages, examples of which we can still admire today in the many fine monasteries and churches with their splendid frescoes, filled with a unique power and sense of the divine glory. The greatest and most noble figures of Serbian monasticism also emerge during this period, and one may well measure the blessedness of an age by the number of saints that it produces.

Superficial observation suggests that throughout the Middle Ages the Serbian Church was subordinate to secular authority, but the archbishops were the leaders of the Church *together* with the rulers, just as the rulers and the archbishops *together* were the leaders of the State. "Every Serbian ruler, by his theological training and his feelings for the Orthodox Church, could have been a worthy leader of it; and, vice versa, every archbishop, by his love for his people and country and his political gifts, could have been a worthy ruler of the State." [11] A shining example of this is St. Sava himself, who was equally an ascetic who had turned away from the world, a distinguished theologian and an energetic organizer of ecclesiastical, cultural and social life. As a skillful statesman and politician he was the founder of the ecclesiastical independence of Serbia and co-founder of its political autonomy.

Rastko Nemanjic, St. Sava's family name, was a prince of the ruling family of Serbia, Nemanya. Members of the royal family were often active in the Church as well; for example, Predislav, the son of King Uros I, became Sava II, Bishop of the Serbian Church in 1263. Many kings gave up their thrones and became monks and saints. Stefan Nemanya, St. Sava's father,

---

[11] R. Josić, "Srpska pravoslavna crkva na medij Istoka i Zapada u Srednjem veku," in *Glasnik službeni list srpske pravoslavne crkve,* 10, 11, 12 (Belgrade, 1964), p. 224.

patron of the monastery of Studenitsa and many others, died in
1200 as the holy monk Simeon. Sava's mother took the veil as
the nun Anastasia. Even Sava's brother, King Stefan Prvovencani,
an outstanding ascetic theologian, became a monk before his
death. The list could easily be continued, which is why Archbishop Danilo II wrote his book at the beginning of the 14th
century about the kings and church leaders of the Serbian people.
He wanted to "sing worthy hymns of praise to those who have
loved Jesus", for these men were "splendid examples for all
who saw them". Danilo describes their lives so that it may "show
the way of life to those who love God".[12] This praise is all the
more justified inasmuch as the Serbian rulers regarded it as
their first duty ". . . to make the Serbian people a People of
God".[13] Hence the words "Render to Caesar the things that are
Caesar's" were not taken by the Serbian Church as an injunction to do no more than was necessary, but rather as a command
to help the State inasmuch as it is concerned to create and
maintain safety and freedom for men.[14] Thus the third feature
of the medieval Serbian Church is harmonious cooperation with
the secular power to further the well-being of the flock entrusted
to it, the Serbian people.

IV

THEOSIS AND COMMUNITY LIFE

Serbian Orthodox theology sees a further characteristic of the
Church as life in community, both the "being one" (Jn. 17, 21f.)
of the faithful among themselves, and the union of the faithful

[12] Danilo II, *Životi kraljeva i archiepiskopa srpskih* (ed. L. Mirković)
(Belgrade, 1935), pp. 5-7.
[13] Domentianus, *op. cit.,* pp. 52, 54.
[14] In spite of his work for the State, Sv. Sava is opposed to war. When
war threatens he does all he can to avert it by prayer and mediation. If
war still comes he warns the generals "not to fight without justice . . .
for every man will be arraigned for his misdeeds at the Last Judgment".
Cf. Theososius, "Život svetog Save," in *Stare srpske biografije* (ed. Bašić)
(Belgrade, 1924), pp. 163, 200ff., 217.

with Christ as individuals and as a community. Like the union of man and woman in one flesh, the Church will be united with Christ (Eph. 5, 31f.) and share in his glory. Here we meet the idea, which runs through all patristic theology of theosis, namely, the divinization of the creature and the Church, which, however, "will be perfected only at the end of time, after the resurrection. Nevertheless, this divinizing union must start in this world. . . ." God has "given us, in the Church, all the objective requirements, all the means . . . to reach this goal. So, for our part, we must now fulfill the necessary subjective requirements, for union is achieved in 'synergy', in the cooperation of man with God".[15] These words of Vladimir Lossky state one of the main ideas of medieval Serbian Orthodox theology. They emphasize that theosis means fusion with the love of God, and as Christ was the shepherd, so there must also be a theosis of the flock: "The divine love for man . . . was the power which brings together those who turn to God in love and seek eternal goods in a com-munity of common life and action. Through the latter it is possible to bear in common the weaknesses of one's brother, to enjoy in common the gifts of the Holy Spirit, to realize in com-mon the individual and collective image of God and, in common with Christ, to pass into the kingdom of heaven." [16]

These ideas were particularly important for the spirituality of the monastic communities of this time, but also for the whole Serbian people. The aim of the Serbian Church and the Serbian rulers was to attain this goal: to give to the people "all the objective requirements" (Lossky). This is expressed clearly in the words of St. Sava when he is speaking about himself and his father, King Stefan Nemanya: ". . . if we prove ourselves before Christ as good shepherds and look after the vineyard entrusted to us, we shall receive double grace and gifts from God: not only because of the deeds we shall do, but also because of those that our flock will do following our example." [17]

[15] V. Lossky, *Die mystische Theologie der morgenländischen Kirche* (Graz, 1961), p. 250.
[16] Sv. Sava, *op. cit.*, footnote 8, chs. 17-19.
[17] Domentianus, *op. cit.*, pp. 49, 52.

Thus the theosis of the Christian in and with the Church is achieved, on the one hand, through the "divine love for man which has acted in Christ" and which brings about union with Christ and with one another, and, on the other, through "synergy, co-operation with God" (Lossky). Man's contribution to this synergetic activity is, according to the Serbian sources, his love of God. That means giving all one's love to one's neighbor and having the right faith in relation to God. Love for one's neighbor was not just a matter for the Church and for pious monks, as is witnessed by figures such as King Stefan (St. Simeon), King Stefan Prvovenčani, Dragutin the ascetic, Milutin and many others. Of King Milutin, the "giver of givers", who built the priceless royal church at Studenitsa in 1314, it is said: "He built many churches, more than anyone else, and made many foundations. At night he visited the poor in disguise and gave them alms. . . . He built hospitals and rest homes for the sick and the old to make their life easier." [18]

The other aspect of synergetic action is holding the "right faith", which is preserved through the Holy Spirit within the community of the apostles and all who are part of this community. The Serbian manuscripts refer constantly to the necessity of right belief for theosis. Only in right belief in the right glorification can one know God, see him and be united with him. This Orthodox faith was formulated and proclaimed by the bishops in common at the seven ecumenical councils, for ". . . all bishops are alike, because they have received the grace of God in equal measure". [19]

Here we see the soteriological character of the Church in its development and presentation of the faith necessary for salvation. In medieval Serbian theology there is particular emphasis on the doxological character of the Church, which is based on the double meaning of the word "orthodoxy". *Doxa* does not only mean "belief", but also "glory", "glorification". Hence the

[18] Danilo II, *op. cit.*, pp. 97ff.
[19] S. Troicki, "Sveti Sava veliki borac za jedinstvo pravoslavnog sveta," in *Glasnik službeni list srpske pravoslavne crkve* (Belgrade, ¹1958), p. 12.

Orthodox Church sees itself not only as the "right-believing", but also as the "right-praising" Church. This conception is clearly expressed in the description of the Serbian Church as *pravoslava,* for *"slava"* means primarily "fame", "honor", "glory". Therefore the right faith, founded on the councils, is also the right glorification of God.

If there were space, one could discuss many other points. As a final summary, however, we can say that the theology of the medieval Serbian Church also failed to work out a clear definition of the Church, but was concerned rather to show the essential criteria of true Church life. Its theological view was strongly influenced by the situation of the Serbian people in the Middle Ages. Certain elements emerged into the foreground and received special emphasis, in contrast with the Byzantine Church. The origin of the existence of the Church is seen as the love of God which is realized in it through Christ, for "Christ is God's love". Thus, the Church as the body of Christ is a body of love. This conception is held in all the areas of the medieval Serbian Church. It determines its eschatological attitude, for one wants "to be where the love of God (Christ) is". From it follows the attitude to the secular power, in common with which one seeks to mold the entrusted flock into a "People of God". By the revelation of God's love among us and by the divinization of human nature in Christ, the way to theosis has been opened to man. Not only the individual can create again in himself the likeness to God, which was destroyed in Adam and raised up again in Christ, but also the community by shaping itself to become the body of Christ. God's love for man determines also the relation of men to one another, because Christians pass on the love given to them to their neighbors.[20] Finally, God's love for man causes man to shine back in love toward God and give him in the right faith (orthodoxy) the right glorification (orthodoxy).

[20] Sv. Sava, *op. cit.,* footnote 8, chs. 33, 38.

PART II
BIBLIOGRAPHICAL
SURVEY

Roger Aubert/*Louvain, Belgium*

Recent Literature on the Modernist Movement

Following the appearance in 1929 of the standard work by Jean Rivière, *Le modernisme dans l'Eglise*[1] and the brief controversy surrounding the publication, two years later, of the *Mémoires* by Loisy,[2] the modernist movement has received little attention for almost a quarter of a century.[3] Recently there has been a sudden and general revival of interest in the subject, and a point of special importance to the historian is that documents which have been long unavailable are now beginning to appear. These texts shed new light on and add new shades of meaning to previous knowledge about the crisis that shook the Roman Church in the first years of the 20th century.

This development began in 1951 with the publication of

[1] This work is still of fundamental importance as a basic account but it has become outdated on numerous points, in reference to which recent publications have supplied information that the author was unaware of. Jean Rivière shows imperfect understanding of the real part played by men like Blondel and von Hügel; in addition, he tends to view the overall crisis as they did in Msgr. Batiffol's Toulouse circle, which, to say the least, would appear to be one-sided. (See E. Amann's review in *Revue sc. rel.* 10 (1930), pp. 676-92, and E. Poulat's remarks in *Histoire, dogme et critique dans la crise moderniste* (Paris-Tournai, 1962), pp. 41, 289-92.

[2] Paris, 1930-1931. See in particular M. J. Lagrange, *Loisy et le modernisme* (Paris, 1932).

[3] Mention should be made, however, of the evocative account by the Anglican canon, Alec Vidler, *The Modernist Movement in the Roman Church* (Cambridge, 1934).

Michael de la Bédoyère's biography of Baron von Hügel, a man referred to by some as "the lay bishop of the modernists". The baron had played a vitally important part in bringing together progressive Catholics, regardless of disciplines and national boundaries. These Catholics had been attempting in a groping fashion to adjust traditional beliefs—or at least ways of expressing them—to the new needs of a world in which culture, mental equipment and intellectual techniques were clearly undergoing a complete transformation.

More recently, a number of works have brought up to date our knowledge of the Italian modernist movement, long neglected because it was thought to be mainly derivative from Loisy or Tyrell or even Laberthonnière, and consequently of little interest. But it is the French modernist movement, on both the exegetical and philosophical fronts, that has recently given rise to several publications of major importance.

THE MODERNIST CRISIS IN FRANCE: ALFRED LOISY

In the course of the detailed research that he undertook to produce a complete documentation of the modernist crisis in France up to the publication in 1907 of the encyclical *Pascendi,* M. Emile Poulat rightly decided on the immediate inclusion in the dossier of an "item vital to the understanding of the controversies". That essential item was *Vie de Loisy,* written by another modernist, Albert Houtin, who was a close friend of Loisy's in the crucial years. Poulat also included a critical study by Félix Sartiaux on Loisy's scientific work as a whole.[4] Sartiaux's work sheds unexpected light on the circumstances in which Loisy produced his *Mémoires,* which emerge looking much more like an artificial reconstruction of his religious development. The book also gives a clear account of Houtin's personal relations

---

[4] *Alfred Loisy, sa vie, son oeuvre, par A. Houtin et F. Sartiaux,* a manuscript annotated and published together with a bibliography on Loisy and a bio-bibliographical index, by E. Poulat (Paris, Éd. du C.N.R.S., 1960).

with Loisy. Houtin and Sartiaux's combined testimony, despite its bias as the work of two disappointed admirers, sheds new light on Loisy's personality. What emerges most clearly is the touchiness, short temper, vindictiveness and pitiless egocentricity of this desk-bound intellectual, not to mention his vanity over honors in the intellectual sphere, his taste for extremely flexible formulas of compromise and, above all, his special capacity for assimilation and adaptation rather than creation.

In addition to a complete bibliography of Loisy's writings, Poulat has included an extremely useful bio-bibliographical index containing nearly five hundred names of people who were in one way or another connected with the modernist crisis. The index is of much greater interest than what we learn from the texts Poulat has edited and will prove to be a valuable aid to study for all those concerned with the history of the French Church in the first third of the 20th century.

However, Poulat has produced a second book on Loisy worthy of even greater attention, *Histoire, dogme et critique dans la crise moderniste,* which summarizes two of the most important works published in France in the heat of the controversy: *Histoire et Dogme* (1904) by Maurice Blondel and *Dogme et critique* (1907) by Edouard Le Roy. Poulat has left over to a subsequent volume the study of the controversy that centered on Le Roy in the years 1905 to 1907. In the first volume,[5] the only one to have come out at the time of this writing, the author has confined himself to the study of what he calls the "Loisy cycle", i.e., the chain reaction between 1902 and 1904 set off by the publication of two little red books in which the French exegete Loisy attempted, on the basis of a critical study of the books of the New Testament, to reformulate some of the basic issues of fundamental theology. Among these issues were the nature of divine revelation and faith that is its counterpart, the limits of

[5] In the collection *Religions et sociétés* (Paris-Tournai: Casterman, 1962). We should like to draw attention to the importance and high quality of the appendix on "Pseudonymes et anonymes modernistes", pp. 621-77, in which, following an objective examination of this phenomenon's significance, a large number of them are identified.

the evolution of dogma, and permanence and contingency in ecclesiastical institutions.

Trained in sociological methodology, Poulat has treated his subject as an "imaginary dialogue", and he strives to reproduce the antiphony of opinion and counter-opinion to which Loisy's revolutionary publications gave rise in the Catholic world. The interest of this work is further enhanced by the author's exploratory search through public and private archives, both in France and abroad, which enabled him to compile a documentation as nearly complete as is possible.

The first two parts consist of a clear, accurate analysis of the basic text, *The Gospel and the Church* (London, 1908), and of the complementary manifesto, *Autour d'un petit livre*, published the following year; they show us the beginnings of the "theological uproar" sparked by Loisy's stand in a number of extremely delicate fields, fields in which even the most liberal Catholics had up till then avoided committing themselves. The reaction of most Catholic publicists and theologians was negative in varying degrees. But there were a number of Catholic intellectuals, especially among younger clergy, who were aware of the urgent need to search for a way of reconciling the faith, to which they wished to remain loyal, with the demands of modern thought which forced them to reconsider certain aspects of traditional orthodoxy.

Parts III and IV set out the various reactions of these "progressives". From p. 270 to p. 277 the author outlines the mentality in the seminaries around 1900. Drawing on unpublished recollections he then movingly portrays (pp. 296-315) two young scholar priests, Fr. Morel and Fr. Vénard, who, "however far they went in criticism, never seem to have wavered in their faith". Pages 364-92 are given over to Batiffol and the group in the Toulouse Institut Catholique. Though Batiffol favored the introduction of critical methods in ecclesiastical science, he opposed Loisy in a heavy-handed manner which the author perhaps judges too severely.

The whole of the fourth part is devoted to bringing to life

again the controversy about the demonstrability of the supernatural by the historical method. This controversy involved three men who were drawn together by their common concern for *aggiornamento* and the reconciliation of faith with the modern mentality. On the one hand there was Fr. Frémont, associated with all that could be called "liberal" in the French Church of the period, but who was unable to grasp the full implications of the problems involved, owing to an oversimplified vision derived from his scholastic formation. On the other hand there was his friend, Fr. Birot, and Bishop Mignot of Albi, one of the rare French hierarchs at the beginning of the 20th century who appears not to have been completely unaware of the intellectual changes of the time and of the parallel politico-religious upheavals. The seventy pages Poulat devotes to these three men— material drawn mainly from abundant correspondence—are among the most evocative in this book so full of evocative pages, for they pinpoint all that was most attractive to intelligent and progressive priests in Loisy's theories of 1902, even though these theories were subsequently to be developed by their author in a way incompatible with the Catholic faith.[6]

The sixth part is also of considerable interest, for it deals with the debate between Loisy and Blondel on the relationship of history to dogma. We will have more to say about this debate later.

In considering a work of this size which deals with so many major questions, inevitably one cannot be in agreement with the author on all points. The main criticism it seems necessary to make is of the consequences flowing from the author's choice

[6] Even at that time, however, Fr. Birot, and many others with him, believed that the blanket condemnation of the modernist movement in the encyclical *Pascendi* was heavy-handed, to say the least. Let the reader peruse these significant lines: "I submit to the encyclical with a sad heart, for its sharp doctrinal severity is constructed on the most artificial of misunderstandings. This severity applies the same reproof and anathema to both friends and foes, and the doctrine which emanates from it is purely negative as regards honest thought. The pope is like an artillery colonel high on a ridge who bombards both armies down on the plain as they grapple in the thick of battle and thus wipes out his own best troops" (p. 443).

of angle, i.e., the sociological angle. Poulat has been so successful in turning himself into the observer and contemporary
recorder of the debates described that he remains too enmeshed
in topical events. Not only does he fail to make sufficient use of
the advantages conferred on the historian by distance in time
but, what is more serious, he hardly gives any idea of the social
and intellectual humus in which the controversies germinated,
i.e., their historical context. It is not enough merely to dissect
patterns of thought and structures; it is equally important to
set thinkers in their actual environment. Only in this perspective
does the history of ideas, if it is to be real history, take on its
full depth.[7]

Having said this, it must be admitted that Poulat's study is
of a remarkably high quality and constitutes the most substantial
contribution yet put at the disposal of historians of the French
modernist movement. It should also be pointed out that, although
the author's sociological preoccupations result in certain limitations, on the other hand these same preoccupations frequently
endow him with interpretive insight from which any historian
could profit. The sociology of religious knowledge is valuable
and even indispensable in attempting to understand the modernist
crisis, the complex and sometimes ambiguous psychology of the
modernists, and the certain lack of understanding shown them
by their opponents. In dealing with a question that all too often
prompts the theologians to analyze and contrast formulas, it is
vitally important to be aware of the "amazing malleability of
religious consciousness", and of what the true nature of Christian
faith *is* in terms of psychological reality and not just as defined
in the manuals.

MAURICE BLONDEL'S REACTION

The biblical question and the problems raised by the historical
and critical study of the origins of Christianity were among the

[7] This criticism has been further elaborated by P. Sorlin in *Revue d'histoire moderne et contemporaine* 10 (1963), pp. 157-8.

burning questions of the modernist crisis. But the crisis also took shape on a more speculative level; moreover, there were passionate discussions among philosophers and theologians who were anxious to remain Catholic but dissatisfied with the traditional solutions to the various problems raised by analysis of religious knowledge and by apologetic methods.

A small and excellent work[8] has recently been added to the other studies already extant on one or another of these questions. It deals with the controversy on miracles started by Maurice Blondel in 1896 which went on with various ups and downs for some fifteen years. The author sets the various stages of this controversy in chronological order and provides a clear and objective summary of the points of view expressed. He notes the strong and weak elements in each new position and then gradually attempts to cull positive material toward a renewal of the concept of miracle and a renewal of its apologetic implications. Although the book is theologically orientated, it should nevertheless be read with interest and profit by historians who will in addition be appreciative of the general outline of French apologetics at the end of the 19th century which is presented in the form of an introduction.

By far the most noteworthy contribution in this field over the last ten years has been the publication of correspondence between Maurice Blondel and various important people directly involved in the modernist controversies, whether actively, as observers, or as adjudicators, in the first decade of the century. The first of these collections of letters to be published was that between Blondel and one of his closest followers, the Jesuit Auguste Valensin,[9] written from 1899 to 1912. Besides adding

[8] F. Rodé, "Le miracle dans la controverse moderniste," in *Théologie historique* 3 (Paris: Beauchesne, 1965). Several similar accounts were produced in the 1950's as Gregorian University doctorate theses. We would like to draw particular attention to P. de Haes, *La résurrection de Jésus dans l'apologétique des 50 dernières années* (Anal. Greg., LIX) (Rome, 1953), and da Vega Coutinho, *Tradition et histoire dans la controverse moderniste, 1898-1910* (Anal. Greg., LXXIII) (Rome, 1954).

[9] Maurice Blondel-Auguste Valensin, *Correspondence (1899-1912)* (2 vols.) (Paris: Aubier, 1957). A third volume has recently appeared: *Ex-*

to our knowledge of Blondel's thought and even more of his soul, these letters are packed with details highly relevant to religious history in the modernist period.

The usefulness of this book is further enhanced by the abundant annotation provided by an anonymous editor. We now know that this editor was the Rev. Henri de Lubac, who thus put to advantage the retreat forced on him by overconscientious censors. The annotation mainly consists of extracts from letters between Blondel and other correspondents—notably Fr. J. Wehrlé, Fr. H. Bremond, Fr. F. Mourret of St. Sulpice, Fr. P. Laberthonnière and Baron von Hügel—which had been preserved in the abundant Blondel archives at Aix-en-Provence. The annotation alone makes these two volumes "an invaluable aid to the study of this period".[10]

Fr. de Lubac rightly points out in the preface that while these texts make clear Blondel's moderate but courageous opposition to conservative moves, they "shed light on the part played from the very beginning by Maurice Blondel in the struggle against the modernist movement, a much stronger and more effective part than is generally recognized". Blondel's antimodernist activity is fully explored in a second publication, *Au coeur de la crise moderniste, le dossier inédit d'une controverse.*[11] This book, consisting of correspondence from 1902 to 1905 between Blondel, Loisy, von Hügel and some others, shows the reader the buildup toward the well-known article *Histoire et dogme.* In these the philosopher from Aix was at pains to demonstrate the weakness of the revolutionary theories put forward by Loisy in his little "red books" and to outline a solution to the real difficulties they raised.

However, Poulat has criticized the way these texts were published[12] and what he says is not without foundation. In any event,

---

traits de la correspondence de 1912 à 1947 (Paris, 1965). This volume deals with a period subsequent to the modernist crisis in the strict meaning of the term.

[10] E. Poulat, *Revue belge de philologie et d'histoire* 41 (1963), p. 1164.

[11] Paris: Aubier, 1960.

[12] See *Revue belge de philologie et d'histoire* 41 (1963), p. 1165, and *Histoire, dogme et critique* . . . , pp. 15, 40-1, 514-15 (footnote 4), 587 (footnote 24), 591 (footnote 30).

the reader would be well advised to make parallel use of *Le dossier* and the last part of *Histoire, dogme et critique,* for Poulat as usual provides summaries of the often long and confused texts of the various correspondents, including printed articles for which *Le dossier* only gives references. Poulat gives a more objective picture of the development of the controversy by describing its incidents in strictly chronological order, by drawing on all the documents known at the time of writing, and by reacting against the one-sided exposition which in places became an unreserved defense of Blondel's point of view.

Poulat gives a clear idea of the complexity of the problems tackled. He shows how Blondel, prone to the habitual difficulty of philosophers when called upon to see things in a historian's perspective and too easily confusing historicity with the historical approach, did not always grasp the exact implications of the difficulties brought out by Loisy. He shows that, on the contrary, a person like von Hügel, more sensitive to historical method, was immediately aware of what was at stake. Nevertheless it seems to me that Poulat has been too hard on Blondel. In his place I would have brought out the undeniable limitations of Blondel's reply, but I would have put far greater stress on the exceptional insight with which he immediately understood the ambiguity of the positions taken up by Loisy and with which he set the delicate problem of tradition on the way toward a solution which today seems in many ways strikingly modern.

The collection of *Lettres philosophiques* that came out in 1961[13] is of less direct influence to the historian of the modernist movement. However, the same cannot be said for the selection of letters between Blondel and Laberthonnière spanning the period 1894 to 1924.[14] In the case of this latter collection of letters, too, the editor has intended to restrict his choice to texts of philosophical interest and to systematically exclude everything concerning facts and people. However, besides what we learn

---

[13] Paris: Aubier, 1961. Addressed to some forty different correspondents, these letters cover the period 1886-1913.

[14] *Maurice Blondel, Lucien Laberthonnière. Correspondance philosophique* (ed. C. Tresmontant) (Paris: Éd. du Seuil, 1961).

about Laberthonnière, on whom the judgments are often super-ficial, there is a good deal to be gleaned from this volume on the religious history of the time, especially in chapter II: *Autour de la crise moderniste*. This book includes other letters on Loisy, and on Blondel's disagreements with von Hügel about him, which may be read as a useful complement to *Lettres philoso-phiques*. Besides somewhat severe comments by Blondel on Edouard Le Roy's article *Qu'est ce qu'un dogme?*, the book also includes a host of details on the two friends' close collabora-tion, following Laberthonnière's resumption of the editorship of *Annales de philosophie chrétienne*. (Several articles published by Blondel under a pseudonym have now been definitely identified.)

Other manuscripts of Blondel's have been published, but they do not directly deal with the period of the modernist move-ment.[15] The texts we have mentioned far from exhaust the data that the Blondel archives provide on the modernist period, but they already considerably help us toward a better knowledge and, above all, understanding of the part Blondel played in the crisis. At that time he was the object of much unjust suspicion and passionate attack, but today we are in a better position not only to understand with what intensity of faith and spirituality he approached and painfully lived through the crisis, but also the way in which his teaching, his writings and his advice were to many wavering souls a tower of strength which saved them from disaster. It is to the everlasting credit of this great Christian that, faced with the unleashed pack who scented heresy, he did not retreat from his perilous task.[16]

[15] I have given a cursory idea of these in *Revue Nouvelle* 42 (1965), pp. 589-97.

[16] It is heartening to see a journal whose line is integrist today honestly admitting that "the philosopher Maurice Blondel has been the victim of a prolonged, grave and terrible injustice" (*Itinéraires* 17 [Nov., 1957], p. 49).

THE MODERNIST MOVEMENT IN ENGLAND:
FRIEDRICH VON HÜGEL

It was in France that the modernist movement provoked the fiercest intellectual battles, but another important center of the movement was in England around the ex-Jesuit, George Tyrrell, and Baron von Hügel. Tyrrell's personality and ideas have not given rise to any important publication since the last war, but the same cannot be said for von Hügel who played an extremely important part in the wings of the modernist movement. He sympathized with the basic aims of the movement in its beginnings but never fell into the modernist heresy as defined by the encyclical *Pascendi*.[17] Thus his principal contribution was to establish contact among various French, English, Italian and German progressives who were all groping in the same direction. He regarded many of them as something more than just the stimulating thinkers they were; to him they were also very dear friends for whom he did all he could to understand and help with an incomparable tact and breadth of vision. The support the baron thus gave the main leaders of the modernist movement earned him a harsh assessment by the first Catholic historians of the movement. A much needed rehabilitation is presently under way.

As early as 1935, N. Nédoncelle had understood how up-to-date and sometimes prophetic the baron's religious philosophy was, and he produced a sensitive and informed study, *Baron Friedrich von Hügel. A Study of His Life and Thought* (London, 1937). But von Hügel's life and work continued to be little known. Since 1951 an excellent biography of him has been available, compiled by Michel de la Bédoyère.[18] The numerous

[17] He was later to define the dividing line between the real modernists and those who sympathized with the movement but remained Catholic in these terms: "The main and decisive difference now seems to me to be the difference between religion conceived of as a merely intra-human phenomenon, not evidential beyond the aspirations of the human race, and religion conceived of as essentially evidential and metaphysical, the effect on us of something greater than ourselves" (Letter of July, 1921, from *Selected Letters*, pp. 333-4).

[18] *The Life of Baron von Hügel* (London: Dent & Sons, 1951).

unpublished texts quoted in this work of synthesis make it a mine of information on the vicissitudes of the modernist movement in several European countries and in Rome, for the baron had feelers everywhere. But the main interest of the book, which sheds new light particularly on the baron's youth, lies in the way it brings us to a better understanding of the subject's personality and confirms the extent to which the baron always steered clear of the religious subjectivism and immanentism of several of his friends.

More recently, Jean Steinman has produced another biography of von Hügel [19] which draws on no new sources but, as the title indicates, stresses the baron's capacity for friendship and his untiring devotion to his friends. In places the book is almost a panegyric, but it at least has the virtue of highlighting what was perhaps the most characteristic trait of von Hügel's rich personality, that is, his openness to all true values and his concern that none should be lost. This explains his determination never to break off relationships but to maintain contact even with those who seemed to him to have gone too far in their exclusivism; as he saw it, such persons were useful in drawing attention to an aspect of the truth or to a real problem to which one had no right to shut one's eyes.

THE ITALIAN MODERNIST MOVEMENT

Several monographs have come out over the past few years in Italy on various major and minor figures in the modernist movement.[20] A good biography[21] has been done of Salvatore Minocchi,

[19] *Friedrich von Hügel, sa vie, son oeuvre et ses amitiés* (Paris: Aubier, 1962). The work is sadly marred by frequent carelessness and inaccuracy with detail. It often fails to delve deeply into things. Nevertheless, this book makes available in French a good and intelligently written introduction to the subject.

[20] Fuller information on this subject is available in the excellent report published by P. Scoppola, *Rivista di storia e letterature religiosa* I (1965), pp. 300-08.

[21] A. Agnoletto, *Salvatore Minocchi. Vita e opere (1869-1943)* (Brescia, 1964).

a priest and the founder of the journal *Studi religiosi*. Its author was able for the first time to use correspondence kept by Minocchi's family and the first version of his *Mémoires,* which is extremely revealing as to his early years (in particular his forced vocation); it also sheds light on life in the seminaries and on the training of the clergy in Italy at the end of the 19th century. The main conclusion from this study is that Minocchi, like Turmel in France, must be considered not so much as a modernist—i.e., someone who believes he can honestly combine faithfulness to the Church with an intellectual position in opposition to traditional orthodoxy—but rather a rationalist who, while well aware of the incompatibility of the Catholic faith with the outcome of his critical research, attempted to conceal this divorce as long as possible so as to safeguard his ecclesiastical position.

There is still no really exhaustive study of Ernesto Buonaiuti, one of the most prominent figures in the Italian modernist movement. Some ten years ago he was the subject of two books, one by the Jesuit, Domenico Grasso,[22] and the other by the Waldensian, V. Vinay.[23] Up to a point these two books complement each other, for the first stresses the theological side while the second goes into Buonaiuti's politico-social activities. However, though of some value, both books are superficial and too greatly colored by their respective author's ideological positions. A new edition of Buonaiuti's memoirs was recently published.[24] The edition includes some very useful annotations and an introduction by A. C. Jemolo in his customarily enlightening and evocative style. However, one might take issue with him for having partly reinterpreted the Buonaiuti of the modernist period in terms of the later and more relaxed Buonaiuti whom he knew and was fond of in the inter-war period.

Romolo Murri's complex intellectual personality has frequently been presented in much too schematic a form, and no definitive biography has yet been done of him, for much of the source ma-

---

[22] *Il cristianesimo di E. Buonaiuti* (Brescia, 1953).

[23] *E. Buonaiuti e l'Italia religiosa del suo tempo* (Torre Pellice, 1956).

[24] M. Niccoli, *E. Buonaiuti: Pellegrino di Roma, la generazione dell'esodo* (Bari: Laterza, 1964).

terial is still inaccessible. In the meantime he has been made the subject of a general study which aims at being a new contribution[25] toward such a definitive biography. The work is mainly important for the period of Murri's life subsequent to the modernist crisis, the period about which up till now the least has been known.

In spite of its very general title, Michele Ranchetti's *Cultura et reforma religiosa nella storia del modernismo*[26] fits best into the monograph category, for the book turns out to be not a work of synthesis on this fascinating subject but a series of portraits of the main leaders of the movement. Many points of deep insight are made, especially about the Milanese group *Rinnovamento* (pp. 191-226), but they are mixed in with other much more debatable points which bear witness to a far too schematic and *a priori* conception of both the modernist movement and "modern thought".

Of far greater interest is Pietro Scoppola's very recent book *Crisi modernista e rinnovamento cattolico in Italia.*[27] Without claiming to be a complete history of the Italian modernist movement, it presents certain essential aspects of the movement with great clarity and combines a broad, general perspective with the presentation of new texts, which up till now have jealously been kept secret.

Catholic intellectuals in the peninsula felt the need for a renewal more than people elsewhere. The renewal was made necessary both by the void left by the "cultural stagnation" that resulted from many people's frightened, negative reaction to the liberal revolution, and by the aspiration toward greater spiritual freedom which for two generations had been gaining ground in

[25] G. Cappelli, *Romolo Murri. Contributo per una biografia* (Collana di storia del movimento cattolico, 16) (Rome, 1965).

[26] Torino: Einaudi, 1963.

[27] Bologna: Il Mulino, 1961. In this short survey it is impossible to go into this or that affirmation of the author or to attempt to develop any of his lines of thought. The following reviews of the book have appeared: D. Grasso, *Civiltà cattolica* (Dec. 15, 1962), pp. 569-74; G. Verucci, *Critica storica* I (1962), pp. 438-44; R. Aubert, *Rev. hist. eccl.* 58 (1963), pp. 644-50; E. Poulat, *Revue belge de philologie et d'histoire* 41 (1963), pp. 1159-62.

circles that were gradually being won over to the new order of things. The first signs of an awakening date from the last years of Leo XIII's reign. No one can deny that this awakening was stimulated by foreign influences, especially by the activities of Baron von Hügel who paid frequent visits to Italy. Nevertheless, the movement had a certain originality of its own that derived from the special position of the Italian Catholic world which for a long time bore traces of the crisis that followed on the Roman Question. The author picks out three mainstreams in this reformist movement: first, there were a few young priests and religious who attempted to react against the backwardness of the ecclesiastical sciences; second, there were the militants in the ranks of the intransigent *Opera dei congressi* who came to see both the organization's practical inadequacies and its theological limitations which they tried to remedy by working out the cultural basis of an authentic Christian democracy; finally, there were the young Catholics who, on the contrary, joined the liberal national stream and tried, from this standpoint, to build a bridge between Catholicism and the aspirations of the modern world.

Apart from the differences of orientation and formation, what is striking when one considers the first group is their common apostolic preoccupation which sets them clearly apart from the majority of the French with whom they made common intellectual cause. They were less concerned with pitting themselves against rationalist and Protestant science than with deepening the religious culture of the average Catholic, for they were well aware of its deficiencies and superficiality.

Murri is, without doubt, the most typical personality in the second group, and the author's interest in him goes back a long way. He is particularly eager to stress the cultural and not merely political and social interest which underlay the activities of this young democratic priest. Murri indeed believed that it was the intellectual immaturity of Italian Catholics and, above all, of the clergy which made it impossible for them to satisfactorily tackle the problems of Christian action in public life.

The focal point of the third group, which was mainly influential in the Milanese area, was the journal *Rinnovamento*. Some of the major subjects discussed in *Rinnovamento* were freedom in scientific research, stress on the subjective position in line with post-Kantian philosophy, the place of the laity in Church life and a new conception of Church-State relations in reaction to the confused thinking of earlier centuries.

Of particular interest in the concluding chapters of the book is the detailed information drawn from unpublished texts on the famous *Convegno di Molveno,* the little "council of European modernism" that met in the summer of 1907 and about which little was previously known. Also of great interest are the pages in which the author attempts to sum up the results of the anti-modernist repression in Italy. He shows that the repression had some positive results, especially insofar as it stimulated social activity, which a number of priests took up as a substitute for the intellectual work which the repression had put out of bounds. All in all, however, the author considers that its results were distinctly negative. Total and brutal as it was, the repression hindered the gradual separation of sound from mistaken elements in the reformist movement; it turned the great mass of the clergy away from pursuing their studies and has further deepened the gulf—of which people were already aware at the end of the 19th century—between the Church and the culture of the time, which today is one of the most serious weaknesses of Catholicism in Italy.

THE ANTI-MODERNIST REPRESSION

Although a general summing up of the anti-modernist repression is now possible fifty years after it happened, the details of its history remain cloudy. Jean Madiran's book *L'intégrisme, histoire d'une histoire*[28] sheds no new light on the matter. The historical chapters (the second section of which resembles a topical pamphlet) attempt to call in question the value of a report published

[28] Paris: Nouvelles Éditions Latines, 1964.

in 1923. The report was based on texts seized during the war in Ghent from the house of the lawyer Jonckx, Benigni's correspondent.[29] Madiran's objective is in itself perfectly justified, for no one could deny that these mysterious documents and the circumstances in which they were published give rise to a variety of problems. But the historian will be disappointed at the way the question is handled. The author ponderously asks questions, the answers to which have long been known. He seems, for example, to be almost completely unaware of the circumstances surrounding the acquisition of the Ghent texts,[30] and he appears to have no notion of the part played by Geurts, a teacher in the Roermond seminary. He refers to some of the texts published by Fr. Antonelli, but his access to them has been entirely secondhand, through an article of Fr. Dulac's, and he borrows the latter's interpretation which sometimes inflates the importance of the texts. Why did he fail to examine the source material which is not that difficult to acquire? The way the author on more than one occasion clearly plays on the meanings of words leaves a very bad taste. For example, he uses a partial refutation to try to refute all the details to be found in a text. A further example: general approbation of an institution with praiseworthy aims is confused with approval for the more than contestable methods to which the institution had secret recourse.

We have mentioned above the work published by Fr. Antonelli. The book consists of a really new batch of texts from the Roman archives that came to light in the course of the examination preceding the beatification of Pius X.[31] Though the author presents the texts as a barrister would present his case file and uses them to further his own thesis, the texts themselves are given in their

[29] This text is known to have been reproduced in 1928 by L. Canet in his book *Saint-Siège, action française et catholiques intégraux* (under the pseudonym N. Fontaine).

[30] Precise details on this are to be found in L. Rogier, *Katholieke Herleving. Geschiedenis van om katholiek Nederland sinds 1853* (Den Haag-Antwerpen, 1957), pp. 447-9.

[31] *Romana beatificationis et canonizationis servi Dei Papae X disquisitio circa quasdam obiectiones modum agendi servi Dei respicientes in modernismi debellatione* (Vatican City, 1950).

entirety and it suffices to apply the rules of historical criticism to them. The reader will find a great deal of information on the much discussed work and personality of Benigni and on the precise nature of Pius X's support for him. The texts also shed light on the pope's attitude to the clergy suspected of holding modernist views, such as the Barnabite Semeria and, more important still, Cardinal Ferrari.

However, in the case of Cardinal Ferrari, the Roman documents only supply one viewpoint and they should be read in conjunction with the evidence collected in the important and recent study by Maria Torresin.[32] Her subtle conclusions deserve our attention, for they confirm what many people, starting with Msgr. Ratti, had already given us to understand: i.e., that on more than one occasion the saintly pope fell victim to an entourage that manipulated him and kept certain documents out of his hands in order to present things to him in a tendentious manner (cf. especially pp. 294-5).

This last example once again shows that history cannot be written in terms of the imagined demands of an ideal order of reality, but that it must be written from the evidence of the documents which are its only solid basis and which sweep away all *a priori* deductions as if they were castles built of playing cards. It is also encouraging that source material in various places, which up till now has been inaccessible, is beginning to be made partially available. It is especially to be hoped that the trend in this direction will continue. Perhaps certain people fear that in making source material available they will scandalize the weak, either by showing certain modernists in a more sympathetic light or by revealing tactical errors committed by the defenders of orthodoxy. Let such people remember that in this matter, as in all others, a Christian should not fear to draw inspiration from the injunction of the gospels: *Veritas liberavit vos.*

[32] "Il cardinale C. Andrea Ferrari, Arcivescovo di Milano e S. Pio X," in *Memorie storiche della diocesi di Milano* 10 (1963), pp. 37-304.

Boris Ulianich / *Bologna, Italy*

Recent Literature on Vatican Council II

Can a Council Be a Failure?

It is impossible in the space of a few pages to consider all the recent literature concerning the Council.[1] Therefore we shall restrict ourselves to some of the problems posed in the literature, particularly from a historical point of view. The Council has

[1] For the enormous bibliography on Vatican Council II, cf. *Arch. Hist. Pontificiae, Eph. Theol. Lov.* and *Rev. Hist. Eccl.* For the most significant panoramas of the various sessions of the Council, cf. G. Caprile, *Il Concilio Vaticano II—Terzo periodo* (Rome, 1965). This is the only volume which has appeared thus far and is a collection of conciliar chronicles previously published in *Civiltà Cattolica*. Also cf. Y. Congar, *Vatican II— Le Concile au jour le jour* (Paris, 1963); *idem, Le Concile au jour le jour —Deuxième session* (Paris, 1964); *idem, Le Concile au jour le jour— Troisième session* (Paris, 1965); G. Lindbeck (ed.), *Dialogue on the Way* (Protestant comments on Vatican Council) (Minneapolis, 1965); R. La Valle, *Coraggio del Concilio—Giorno per giorno la seconda sessione* (Brescia, 1964); *idem, Fedeltà del Concilio—I dibattiti della terza sessione* (Brescia, 1965); H. Helbling, *Das Zweite Vatikanische Konzil— Ein Bericht* (Basel, 1966); R. Laurentin, *L'enjeu du Concile* (Paris, 1962); *idem, L'enjeu du Concile—Bilan de la première session* (Paris, 1963); *idem, L'enjeu du Concile—Bilan de la deuxième session* (Paris, 1964); *idem, L'enjeu du Concile—Bilan de la troisième session* (Paris, 1965); J. Ratzinger, *Die erste Sitzungsperiode des II. Vatikanischen Konzils. Ein Rükblick* (Köln, 1963); *idem, Ergebnisse und Probleme der dritten Konzilsperiode* (Köln, 1965); X. Rynne, *Letters from Vatican City—Vatican Council II (First Session)* (London, 1963); *idem, The Second Session* (New York, 1964); *idem, The Third Session* (London, 1965); E. Schillebeeckx, *Het tweede Vaticans Concilie*, 2 vols. (Den Haag, 1965-66); A. Wenger, *Vatican II, première session* (Paris, 1963); *idem, Vatican II, chronique de la deuxième session* (Paris, 1964); *idem, Vatican II, chronique de la troisième session* (Paris, 1965).

ended. The initial evaluations are beginning to appear while the studies devoted to the fourth session are still being published. There is an immense literature, a real harvest of judgments and new perspectives which already testify of themselves that Vatican Council II is a living council, destined to make an incisive contribution to the ecclesial life of our time. But a council certainly does not work *ex opere operato;* the calling of a council is not enough for the renewal of the Church. At every stage, including the postconciliar, one can raise again the problem debated in 1961 between Schauf[2] and Küng,[3] later reconsidered by Marlé,[4] and recently touched upon again by Bishop Guano,[5] namely: Can a Council be a failure? In effect, as Dom Rousseau writes: "The Spirit only guarantees the infallibility of the Church gathered in council; in no way does it guarantee the impeccability of the fathers who can lack courage and prudence in the application or the non-application of the decrees." [6] For that matter, the history of the Church indicates that a council can also end in failure, either in its working sessions (with regard to the expectations posed to it, and in the sense of a failure to give an exhaustive and timely answer to the problems posed by a particular situation in the Church at a definite time), or also in the execution of its decisions (when these are not implemented, or when they are applied only according to the letter of the law without paying attention to the spirit that sustains and animates them).

[2] In *Kirchenzeitung für das Bistum Aachen* (Aug.-Sept., 1961).

[3] "Kann das Konzil auch scheitern?" in *Rh. Merkur* (Oct. 17, 1961); reproduced in *Kirche im Konzil* (Freiburg, 1963), pp.13-22.

[4] "La réussite du Concile est-elle assurée?" in *Etudes,* 95/373 (1962), pp. 190-95.

[5] "Può fallire il Concilio?" in R. La Valle, *Coraggio del Concilio, op. cit. supra,* footnote 1, pp. 396-400; cf. also M. Gozzini, *Concilio aperto* (Firenza, 1962), p. 9; "Réflexions sur un concile," in *Lum. et Vie* 14 (1965), n. 74, p. 1; P.-A. Liégé, "Le concile de l'espérance," in *Signes du temps* (Jan. 1, 1966), pp. 5-6.

[6] "Vatican II, à partir des conciles précedents," in *Irénikon* 38 (1965), p. 435. Other articles of Dom Rousseau, characterized by profundity and great sobriety, are: "Le deuxième Concile du Vatican. Réflexions ecclésiologiques," in *Irénikon* 35 (1962), pp. 467-78; "Autour du Concile: l'intersession," in *Irénikon* 36 (1963), pp. 204-22; "Chronique de la deuxième session du Concile," in *Irénikon* 36 (1963), pp. 507-27; "Sur la IIIe session du Concile," in *Irénikon* 37 (1964), pp. 508-33; "Chronique de la IVe session du Concile," in *Irénikon* 38 (1965), pp. 473-501.

With respect to the expectations and hopes that were placed in the Council, we can state—and this is generally agreed in the first overall evaluations—that, considered as a whole, they have received a more or less profound hearing in the Council.

Expectations

What was asked of the Council? That it undertake a renewal of the Church; that it complete the decisions of Vatican Council I with the doctrine of episcopal collegiality, inserting this into a more profound ecclesiological context; that it delineate in a more exhaustive manner the place and responsibility of the laity in the Church;[7] that the Church become "really missionary";[8] that, with all due respect to structures proper to the world, it might incarnate itself in the world, animate its structures—in a word, that Christians more decisively engage their resources in the reality of this world, by contributing to the resolution of the world's problems; that the Church better manifest its catholicity, namely, its capacity to respect the diverse civilizations and cultures ("baptizing without westernizing"), its capacity to generate Christ without alienating all the aspirations and values present in them;[9] that, without being a reunion council, it lay the foundations for the unity of all Christians by abdicating whatever form of triumphalism, by admitting the [Roman Catholic] faults in the divisions of the Church, by proclaiming "religious liberty", by recognizing the *de facto* existence of separated Christian communities both in the East and the West, and accepting the consequences deriving from the existence of the ecumenical movement.[10]

[7] O. Roegele, *Was erwarten wir vom Konzil? Gedanken eines Laien* (Osnabrück, 1961).

[8] F. Legrand, *Le concile oecumenique et l'evangelisation du monde* (with a Preface by Cardinal Suenens) (Mulhouse, 1962), p. 142. Cf. also J. D'Souza, "Besoins et exigences des missions aujourd'hui," in *Un Concile pour notre temps* (Paris, 1961), pp. 167-90.

[9] R. Laurentin, *L'enjeu du Concile, op. cit. supra,* footnote 1, p. 158.

[10] *Fragen an das Konzil—Anregungen und Hoffnungen* (Freiburg, 1961), pp. 39ff.; B. Häring, *The Joannine Council, Witness to Unity* (New York, 1963); O. Roegele, *Was erwarten wir vom Konzil?, op. cit. supra,* footnote 7, pp. 35-45; O. Rousseau, "Les espoirs oecuméniques à l'épreuve des réalités," in *Un Concile pour notre temps, op. cit. supra,*

To borrow the title of a very significant collaborative study, one wanted "a council for our time",[11] that is, a council designed for the Church, not a Church detached and distant from the world and its problems, but a "Church in the world", willing to read and accept the "signs of the times" in order to give them an evangelically adequate answer. All of these hopes, these expectations (and we could list a very long series of writings in which the terms "hope" and "expectation" recur) blossomed in the wake of the instructions, requests and motivations given by Pope John XXIII.

The Response: A Pastoral Council

From the day that he announced his intention of convening a council, John XXIII made no secret of the direction in which the Council would have to move. It was also possible to deduce this from the statements of his closest collaborators. On November 7, 1959, "The Tablet" (p. 972) published a statement by Cardinal Tardini in which he affirmed: "This Council is not directed against anyone. Those who have said or written that it plans to condemn persons or movements are mistaken. Rather than condemn, the Council intends to attract those who are outside the Church." In 1960, Cardinal Montini stated that the coming Council would be characterized by a new approach in comparison with other councils.[12] In 1961 Bishop Felici pointed out the pastoral character of the Council.[13] However, the discourses

---

footnote 8, pp. 191-223. Cf. also A. Bea, *The Unity of Christians* (with abundant bibliographical notes) (New York, 1963); H. Küng, *The Council, Reform and Reunion* (New York, 1961); B. Pawley, *Looking at the Vatican Council* (London, 1962); K. Skydsgaard, *The Papal Council and the Gospel* (Protestant theologians evaluate the coming Vatican Council) (Minneapolis, 1961).

[11] *Un Concile pour notre temps* (Paris, 1961). Collaborators in this work were I.-P. Dubois-Dumée, J. De Broucker, R. Voillaume, M.-D. Chenu, M. Marty, F. Houtart, L.-C. Baas, J. D'Sousa, O. Rousseau and Y. Congar.

[12] "I concili ecumenici nella vita della Chiesa—Prolusione al XXXII coeso di aggiornamento culturale—Passo della Mendola—16 agosto 1960," in *Discorsi dell'Arcivescovo di Milano—La Chiesa (1957-1962)* (Milan, 1962), pp. 148ff.

[13] "Orientamenti pastorali del Concilio Ecumenico Vaticano II," in

of Pope John on September 11 and October 11, 1962, mark the real milestones in this direction. The Church is no longer gathered in council in order to condemn and defend itself from outside attack; the Church desires to dedicate itself to a deeply positive task:

> "This certain and immutable doctrine, which must be faithfully respected, must be deepened and presented in a way that responds to the demands of our time. Indeed, the deposit of faith itself, namely, the truths contained in our doctrine, is one thing; something else is the form in which these truths are enunciated [*modus quo . . . enunciantur*] while preserving for them the same sense and the same scope. One must attribute great importance to this formulation and, if necessary, we must patiently insist on its elaboration: that is, ways of presenting these matters must be used which better correspond to the magisterium whose character is preeminently pastoral."

This last proposition is almost never grasped in its full import because the official translations misconstrue the sense of the original Latin text.[14] It is a particularly pregnant text because it discloses not only one of the key dispositions of Pope John, but also because it univocally clarifies the direction which he wanted to imprint on Vatican Council II: the magisterium "has a preeminently pastoral character".

L'Osservatore Romano (Sept. 18-19, 1961), p. 5. Note the following passage: "In the beginning some bishops lamented the fact that a particular pastoral commission was not formed. However, this did not occur through oversight or negligence, but because it was desired that all the commissions would work with a pastoral spirit."

[14] Cf. *Acta Apost. Sedis*, 54 (1962), p. 792. The Latin text reads: ". . . scilicet eae inducendae erunt rationes res exponendi, quae cum magisterio, cuius indoles praesertim pastoralis est, magis congruant." The official Italian translation of this whole passage makes the original text unrecognizable. The official translations in other languages seem to follow suit. The only exact translation of which we are aware is *"in eigener Übersetzung"* by *Herder Korr.*, 17 (Nov. 1962), p. 87. The problem of official translations—and also of the resumés of Pope John's unwritten discourses—undoubtedly merits a study that could prove to be of significant interest.

As early as the spring of 1963, Professor George A. Lindbeck[15] spoke of the end of the Counter-Reformation. This phrase has been repeated to the point of becoming a slogan. It is certainly true that an era in the history of the Church, the Tridentine era, is finished, and we are in the process of unleashing a new period.[16] In effect, principally through its pastoral initiative, Vatican Council II has drawn away from the characteristic typology of all the other ecumenical councils that preceded it. H. Jedin has given a masterful demonstration of this in *Strukturprobleme der ökumenischen Konzilien*:

> "The old division of Council propositions into dogma and discipline, which we observe altogether in four historical types, is hereby overcome from within. In the vision of the pope, the condemnation of errors of faith is not the first task of the Council. It must proclaim the Christian faith to the world and so proclaim it that the world hears its appeal. It must be the whole truth, and not an abbreviation. Preaching and instruction are not the only proclamation, but also worship, *caritas* and pastoral care; the teaching and the life of the Church are part of this proclamation, the witness of Christ in the world, kerygma." [17]

Elements of Perplexity and Complexity

There was no lack of opposition to the action first sketched and then desired by Pope John, especially on the part of the curia and some members of the episcopacy. It has been said that the Roman curia, which virtually controlled the key positions in the preparatory commissions and then in the Council itself, wanted no more than "the approval of the schemas already prepared, eventually with some retouching".[18] One could even say that

[15] Cf. J. Hampe, *Ende der Gegenreformation? Das Konzil. Dokumente und Deutung* (Stuttgart-Berlin-Mainz, 1964), p. 17.

[16] Cf. in this regard the excellent article of G. Alberigo, "The Council of Trent: New Views on the Occasion of Its Fourth Centenary," in *Concilium* 7, pp. 69–87.

[17] Köln und Opladen (1963), p. 20.

[18] H. Jedin, *Strukturprobleme der ökumenischen Konzilien* (1963), p. 15.

curialization reached an apex in this Council, perhaps even more than in Vatican Council I, because of the fusion of important conciliar offices with the curia. There was a tendency to isolate Pope John by incasing his impetus and openness in forms long defined according to the patterns of a closed and apologetic scholastic theology. Among other supporters of the curial line was Cardinal Siri who stated in a conference held in Genoa on "Ecumenical Councils and the Renewal of the Church": "Naturally it is both possible and necessary that the Church renew its defense and its explicitation of the truth against modern errors and confusions." [19] And in an interview published by the weekly *Orizzonti* (October 18, 1962) the same cardinal categorically emphasized the "doctrinal" character of Vatican Council II—naturally, in opposition to "pastoral".

At the basis of the opposition to "pastoral"—of the distinction between "doctrinal" and "pastoral"—there was generally a false interpretation of what the term signified, as if such an initiative by the Council could have led to a sort of "diluted or watered-down theology", to use the expression of Schillebeeckx.[20] Only in this light is it possible to understand certain preliminary statements such as that of S. Tromp in an interview published in *De Gelderlander* (December 18, 1962): "In my opinion the first pastoral obligation is that of transmitting the truth"; or the judgment of Bishop Carli: "Therefore, the very first fulfillment of the *pascite* is the *docete*." [21] However, in our opinion the root of the incomprehension of, and the opposition to, the "pastoral" wanted by Pope John lies, as Schillebeeckx has shown, in a different way of conceiving the truth: essentialistic and non-existential. In this difference of perspective, or outlook on the world, Schillebeeckx believes it is possible to distinguish the deepest differences of the two groups of so-called "progressives" and so-called "conservatives". The first group thinks "existentially", i.e.,

---

[19] *Concilio Ecumenico Vaticano II* (Geneva, 1962), p. 195.

[20] *Die Signatur des zweiten Vatikanums—Rükblick auf drei Sitzungsperioden* (German translation of the original Dutch cited *supra,* footnote 1) (Wien, 1965), p. 54.

[21] *La Chiesa a Concilio* (Milan, 1964), p. 145.

it is open to the living, human, historical reality and understands truth dynamically. For the second group, on the other hand, there exists between themselves and reality, without their being conscious of it, a kind of diaphragm composed of a conceptual world. The essentialist way of thinking treats the mysteries of the faith and of human life as if these were abstract essences which, first of all, have to be formulated in the clearest possible way. Thus, we see how they considered the scope of the Council to be nothing other than a pure and exact formulation of an immutable *essence*. Such an attitude could not fail to have repercussions on all the problems taken up by the Council.[22]

Schillebeeckx's interpretation is very enlightening. However, we think that it can be complemented by another very noteworthy intervention of Chenu in *Un Concile "Pastorale"*.[23] (Because of the brevity of this article we cannot give an adequate review of this work.) According to Chenu the meaning of "pastoral" cannot be reduced to "an appropriate and exact application of speculative theology", as if speculative theology were to develop the principles and pastoral theology draw the conclusions on a concrete level. In clear opposition to this division the Council fathers reacted against the schemas drawn up by the preparatory commissions, judging them abstract, scholastic, not biblical, not pastoral, not ecumenical, in a word, not in line with the directives and program that John XXIII had stated once again in his discourse at the opening of the Council. For Chenu, " *'pastoral'* qualifies a theology; it is a manner of thinking theology and teaching the faith, or better: it is a particular vision of the economy of salvation";[24] "pastoral" means, and is, "the Word of God in action".[25] The word derives from a person, while the doctrine objectifies and depersonalizes; the Word of God derives from the person of the man-God. And the Church gives the world not only

---

[22] Cf. *Die Signatur . . . op. cit. supra*, footnote 20, especially the paragraph concerning "Misverständnisse auf dem Konzil," pp. 64-73.

[23] This first appeared in *Parole et Mission* 21 (April 15, 1963), pp. 182-202, and was then reprinted in *La Parole de Dieu*, II, *L'évangile dans le temps* (Paris, 1964), pp. 655-72. We cite this latter volume.

[24] *Ibid.,* p. 658.

[25] *Ibid.,* p. 661.

a doctrine, but the living Jesus Christ. One cannot separate the doctrine of Christ from the person of Christ. As Chenu remarks: "The realism of the faith proceeds precisely from the fact that it is knowledge of a person-to-person relation, and not the simple docile acceptance of a formal teaching, dogmas to be believed and precepts to be carried out: it has someone as object."

For this reason, the Council's task according to John XXIII's wish was to communicate the Word of God "in its condition of dialogue with man, through and in a Church in state of mission. God speaks *today*":[26] the Word of God proclaimed in time, evangelization bound to the stages of humanity. The necessity of finding a language intelligible to 20th-century men of different cultures, in the midst of a flourishing technological civilization, does not simply respond to a pedagogical exigency, but flows from the necessity to give the Word of God its actuality in history. Thus, the separation of "doctrinal" and "pastoral" must be considered artificial. "Doctrine", understood as a series of abstract principles from which moral applications are deduced, devitalizes evangelization. "Theology", science of God, "is inconceivable except through and in an *'economia'*, that is, through a coming of God in time, prepared in the chosen people, consummated in Christ and now realized in the Church".[27] This means that history becomes a part of the fabric of the kingdom of God. This is quite a different perspective than the poor and pragmatic interpretation of a pastoral theology understood as "the art . . . of grasping and conquering outsiders".[28]

Considered in this light one sees more clearly the significance of the misconstrued translation of the passage in the opening dis-

[26] *Ibid.*, p. 663.

[27] *Ibid.*, p. 666.

[28] L. Carli, *La Chiesa a Concilio* (Milan, 1964), p. 144. However, we would like to add that, apart from the most fruitful notes of both Schillebeeckx and Chenu, there still remains the complexity of the particular situations of certain groups of the Fathers: their formation, their insufficient preparation for dialogue, and almost an inferiority complex that they exhibited when confronted with the organs of the Roman Curia. The two authors mentioned certainly do not deny all these elements. They, as well as many other authors concerned with Vatican Council II, recognize in the opposition a certain utility.

course of the Council in which Pope John stated with respect
to the magisterium that its "character is preeminently pastoral".
In this context it should be mentioned that the personality and
action of John XXIII merit a more profound study. There is a
superficial kind of hagiography which tries to paint a myth of
a good, simple, jovial man who had complete and utter trust in
providence. But such a myth veils and falsifies John XXIII's true
interior physiognomy and the originality—anything but impro-
vised or dilettantish—of the clearly pastoral imprint of his pontificate and of the Council.

In fact, the convening of the Council bearing his signature
(even considered as an impromptu inspiration) is in harmony
with the Johannine synthesis which embraces, writes Cardinal
Lercaro, "the whole Church in its most essential doctrinal and
institutional aspects, challenged by the human problematic of our
time". It is an act performed with "a calculated boldness which,
even though obviously unable to foresee all the details or even
the material contents of certain future developments, nevertheless
substantially grasped the theological and historical nucleus of
the situation of the Church within the span of his pontificate".[29]
But what about the expectations of John XXIII relative to the
Council, and more in general, with respect to the historical and
religious task of our generation? Cardinal Lercaro responds that
if one considers "the major lines of Pope John's thought and his
more general and more original resolutions, if one discerns,
which we believe is possible, his major historical and ecclesiological tenets, and if one attempts to gather from them the global
synthesis of his instruction, then there is a sense, ultimately quite
sincere and rigorous, in which it is possible to say that in spite
of everything they were only at the beginning. . . ." [30]

---

[29] G. Lercaro, *Giovanni XXIII—Linee per una ricerca storica* (Rome,
1965), p. 30. For a masterful profile of Pope John, see Cardinal Suenens'
discourse in the Council, Oct. 28, 1963, in R. La Valle, *Coraggio del
Concilio, op. cit.,* pp. 517-25.

[30] We would agree with Schillebeeckx: "Instead of a transition pope,
he became the pope of a Church in transition" (*"statt eines Übergang-
spapstes [wurde er] zum Papst der Überganskirche"*): *op. cit.,* p. 74.

Gleanings

One of the most important results of the Council is episcopal collegiality which constitutes the *doctrinal foundation* of pastoral renewal. Through the affirmation of this principle, the relations between papacy, episcopacy and curia have been altered from what they were in the past. The reform of the curia, of its structure and functions, and its adequacy to the changed situation have again come under discussion, but now on the basis of a doctrinal principle.[31] Especially since the Council of Trent, the curia had assumed a central position between the pope and the bishops. However, now that the doctrine of the collegial power of the bishops in the Church has been affirmed, the curia must become an executive organ of the pope, and at the same time of the bishops.

The reports concerning the various sessions of the Council, and particularly the third session, reveal very often the difficulties that partisans of the curia introduced in the proceedings of the Council, especially concerning some plans, among which episcopal collegiality is foremost. And the question arises whether, after the Council, the curia will not attempt to retard or pigeonhole those decisions that could be detrimental to its position. We do not have to accept the phrase that Serafian places in the mouth of the curia ("Popes come and go, but we, we who are the Church, are immortal")[32] in order to see the problem of curial bureaucracy. Is it enough to replace some of the personnel without reforming the fundamental structure in order to change the spirit of such a secular institution? This is a problem which has considerable weight for the implementation of the spirit of the Council. Of course the Catholic Church must have appropriate machinery, but "no longer that which promulgated the decrees of the Council of Trent, but that of Vatican Council II".

Happily the institution of an episcopal synod has been empha-

---

[31] E. Schillebeeckx, *Die signatur . . . op. cit.,* p. 113.
[32] M. Serafian, *The Pilgrim* (1964). This work has received much criticism. However, considered with the necessary reservations, it is useful for its reconstruction of the period treated: the second session.

sized as a middle path between the central power and episcopal conferences, but it has also been emphasized that "if by an over-zealous show of strength the central ancien régime succeeds in totally dominating the 'synod', the Council will have been a fail-ure in large part, and some day everything will have to start all over again".[33]

Still another problem was debated in the Council hall itself, namely, the theological qualification of the conciliar decisions. Nor can this fail to become a more decisive question in the com-ing years. In what degree are these decisions binding? In previous ecumenical councils there was a clear distinction between dog-matic and disciplinary decrees: it is enough to recall the Council of Trent and Vatican Council I, although the latter in fact pro-mulgated only dogmatic decrees. The conciliar texts of Vatican Council II, on the other hand, represent a new element in the history of the councils inasmuch as they lack those canons or anathemas on which the norm of interpretation was based in determining what should be considered defined and binding. Thus, even if the question of their binding force is less significant, in comparison with the texts of prior councils, it is bristling with more difficulties than first meet the eye.

Betti has just completed a study of the theological qualification ascribed to the *"Dogmatic" Constitution on the Church*.[34] He maintains that by giving the Constitution the qualification "dog-matic", "the universal magisterium undertakes as such to propose the doctrine contained therein", even if it is not a true and proper definition in the technical sense. Besides, the latter concerns solely the degree of certainty and does not at all affect the au-thenticity of the doctrine taught. Thus, even if it is considered irrevocable as a whole, this doctrine does not prevent the possi-bility of "a further investigation".

---

[33] O. Rousseau, "Vatican II, à partir des conciles précédents," *op. cit.*, p. 447. Cf. also H. de Lubac, "In limine," in *La Chiesa del Vaticano II* (ed. G. Barauna) (Firenze, 1965), p. 5: Eng. tr.: *The Church of Vatican II* (2 vols.) (Chicago, 1966).

[34] "Qualificazione teologica della Costituzione," in *La Chiesa del Vati-cano II, op. cit.*, pp. 267-74.

Ratzinger likewise acknowledges that, with respect to "the measure of its theological obligation", as the expression of the supreme magisterium of the Church (the entire college of the bishops in union with the pope), the text stands "far above the ordinary expressions of the pope's magisterium, inclusive of the papal encyclicals". However—and in this he is in agreement with Betti—that does not mean that "the text is irreformable in the details of its formulations, in the guidelines of its thought, and in its citations of scripture and the Fathers".[35] On the other hand, Congar maintains, albeit with some hesitation, that with respect to the sacramentality of the episcopacy (*Constitution on the Church*, n. 21), while it is not "in manner of expression . . . a dogmatic definition", nevertheless, since "the material is so important and its place in the doctrine of the episcopacy is so decisive . . . it is difficult to admit that the Council did not pronounce a definitive judgment here".[36]

This opinion is clearly rejected by Ratzinger.[37] The doubts and perplexities are understandable in this new sphere which perhaps requires parameters and instruments different from the traditional ones. But it certainly poses a possible danger for the postconciliar period which could establish a particular interpretation of the "pastoral" concept, so that some conciliar texts would be accepted as pastoral—understood in a practical sense—and their supporting doctrine be sought rather in the decisions of previous councils and in the previous pontifical magisterium.

[35] "La collegialità episcopale dal punto di vista teologico," in *La Chiesa del Vaticano II, op. cit.*, p. 759.
[36] "In luogo di conclusione," in *La Chiesa del Vaticano II, op. cit.*, pp. 1262-63.
[37] *Art. cit.*, p. 758.

Heiko Oberman / *Cambridge, Mass.*

From Occam to Luther

A Survey of Recent Historical Studies on the
Religious Thought of the 14th and 15th Centuries

For the advancement of the field of late medieval theology it would be indispensable to have an interpretative survey available of post-World War II developments, consensus and debates. For the present our goal is less ambitious; we exclude all periodical literature and select some recent studies that deserve special attention, either because of the contribution therewith made, or because of the subject matter treated.

For the medievalist and the Reformation scholar alike the paucity of studies in 14th- and 15th-century thought has long been a reason for complaint. The few available studies have often concentrated on a comparison with either Aquinas or Luther to the detriment of an understanding of the integrity of the theological tradition of the period as such. Lately, however, a series of important monographs from a variety of countries and "schools" seems to have marked a turn of the tide.[1]

[1] For a more extensive version of this biographical survey, cf. "Forschungen zum spätmittelalterlichen Theologie," in *Theol. Literat. Zeit.* 91 (1966), n. 6. Here there is a further discussion of B. Smalley, *English Friars and Antiquity in the Early Fourteenth Century* (Oxford, 1960); M. Gilmore, *Humanists and Jurists: Renaissance Studies* (Cambridge, Mass., 1963); J. Dempsey Douglass, *Preaching Justification in the Later Middle Ages* (Leiden, 1966).

I

A prominent and stimulating figure in contemporary scholarship is the Benedictine monk Paul de Vooght. After a number of articles dealing with Huss' relation to Augustine (1946) and Huss' doctrine of the eucharist (1953), de Vooght became more generally known for his presentation of the 14th- and 15th-century discussion of the relation of scriptural and extrascriptural tradition.[2] Of lasting value is doubtlessly the part dedicated to the edition of the interesting first twelve *questiones* of the *Summa* of Gerard of Bologne (d. 1317), but the interpretive section of this book, feeding right into the discussion unleashed in 1956 by Josef Rupert Geiselmann's new interpretation of Trent's decree on scripture and tradition, also proved to be significant both for its broad coverage and ample documentation. Most striking is de Vooght's plea for a positive evaluation of the "orthodox" regard for the *sensus catholicus* by John Wyclif, in an earlier century often regarded as a "forerunner of the Reformation" and as a representative of "the scriptural principle". De Vooght's conclusions will have to be carefully checked in the light of the edition of Wyclif's important early work *De Trinitate*[3] which is an attack on the nominalist thesis that the doctrine of the Trinity belongs to the *pura credibilia*. For Wyclif, this doctrine in the first place is not just *credibilis* but also *intelligibilis*. In the second place, it is not derived from tradition and cannot serve as proof of the complementary nature of tradition *vis-à-vis* scripture. As Wyclif continued to point out throughout his life, it is rather a rational elaboration of the *veritas philosophica* of scripture which we owe to the Doctors of scripture. Wyclif's regard for tradition—as that of the 16th-century Reformers—is determined by the measure of its *elaboratio* of scripture. It is quite clear that the young Wyclif is radically opposed to nominalism on all these debated

---

[2] P. de Vooght, *Les sources de la doctrine chrétienne* (Bruges, 1954).

[3] A. DuPont Breck, *Johannis Wyclif Tractatus de Trinitate* (Boulder, Col., 1962), p. 2: "By natural reason it can be clearly and truly proved that God is threefold." *Ibid.*, p. 11: "It is possible to establish the doctrine of the incarnation—and other doctrines which are much more difficult than the Trinity—without supernatural means." Cf. also pp. 29, 162.

points and cannot possibly be placed with Occam and Gerson in one spiritual family, as de Vooght suggested for the Wyclif of five years later.

In 1960 the same author published two interdependent works on John Huss[4] in which he comes remarkably close to Luther's judgment, according to which Huss is not to be regarded as a proponent of doctrinal *reformation* but rather as one driven by the ideal of moral *reform*.[5] Here Wyclif appears in a completely different and less rosy light, namely, as the evil genius behind the fate of Huss, just as much responsible for Huss' condemnation as d'Ailly (d. 1420) and Gerson (d. 1429). These masterminds behind the process at the Council of Constance against the naive Huss wanted to establish their own orthodoxy at his expense: "They felt the need to reassure themselves as to their own orthodoxy. Thus they grabbed the providential chance to burn a heretic." [6]

De Vooght supports those who claim a greater measure of originality and less subservience of Huss to Wyclif than had been assumed in the last century (J. Loserth!), by pointing to the endemic Czech reform movement (Milic de Kromeriz, d. 1374). The 19th-century conclusion is retained: "Il a tout reçu" (pp. 45, 71); however, Huss derived his ideas not from Wyclif but from this Bohemian reformism. As a matter of fact, compared with the radical Nicholas of Dresden (d. ca. 1418), Huss appears extremely restrained and conservative. In the crucial period of 1415-1418 it is the words of Nicholas with their intricate compound of radical Hussitism and Waldensian ideas which prove to be highly esteemed in the Taborite community.[7]

In view of Huss' early (1397!) admiration, copying and defense of Wyclif, considerable difficulties emerge for de Vooght,

[4] *L'hérésie de Jean Huss* (Louvain, 1960); *Hussiana* (Louvain, 1960).
[5] M. Luther, *WATR* 1, n. 624; cf. n. 880.
[6] *L'hérésie de Jean Huss, op. cit.,* p. 474; *Hussiana, op. cit.,* p. 208.
[7] Cf. the Introduction and the attractive edition of H. Kaminsky (ed.), *Master Nicholas of Dresden: The Old Color and the New. Selected Works Contrasting the Primitive Church and the Roman Church* (Transactions of the American Philosophical Society, New Series V, 1) (Philadelphia, 1965).

perhaps best suggested by quoting one more sentence: "In the depths of his soul, Huss is a divided man. His mentality [esprit] is catholic, but his heart is with Wyclif" (pp. 85, 181, 207, 214). Two examples should suffice to indicate the efforts made to clear Huss from the charge of heresy. As concerns the eucharist, some Prague theologians follow Wyclif in teaching that after the consecration there is still bread on the altar, but whereas they think in terms of the *remanentia* of *material* bread, Huss speaks here about *eucharistic* bread (p. 97; cf. pp. 63, 131, 149, 325). Secondly, there is no trace of Donatism in Huss' thesis that a priest who is not a good Christian is not truly (*vere*) a priest, since after all an evil priest remains a true (*verus*) priest (pp. 175, 271, 303, 462). Huss escapes the pitfalls of Wyclif's sophisms (!) and insists upon the abiding validity of the sacraments administered by the *indigni*.[8]

Although de Vooght speaks degradingly about "the Parisian theologians" who were unable to grasp the distinction between *verus* and *vere* (p. 303), the question arises whether the fathers of Constance were actually rash in their judgment. The use Huss made of this distinction in *De Ecclesia* especially leads to the conclusion that, though de Vooght is justified in defending Huss against the charge of Donatism, we encounter here what we are inclined to call "semidonatism". There is an undertone of traditional antidonatism insofar as moral turpitude of priests does not prevent God from using them as administrants of valid sacraments. At the same time a priest, bishop or pope who lives in a state of sin has lost the power of the keys: "In a state of sin he has not the *plenitudo potestatis* to bind or loose, nor can he convey any spiritual benefit to the Church."[9]

If indeed the truly Christian life (*vere*) had been designated as the private aspect of the canonically ordained (*verus*) priest, Huss' position would have been in keeping with the medieval tradition. Actually the *vere* or quality of a prelate's life is the criterion and constituent factor of his power as a canonically con-

[8] Cf. p. 214; also cf. *Hussiana, op. cit.,* pp. 231-40.
[9] S. Harrison Thomson (ed.), *Tractatus Responsivus* (Philadelphia, 1927), p. 5.

stituted (*verus*) member of the hierarchy: "If the Pope imitates Christ in his life, we believe that he is his true (*verus*) deputy. . . . If not, then he is a representative of the Antichrist. . . ." [10]

II

We have made such elaborate comments on de Vooght's contribution to the field because he touches upon a number of central issues in the 14th, 15th and early 16th centuries. His books are passionately written, and therefore fascinating reading, but they tend on the other hand to divide the cast into heroes and villains. One of the chief victims of this procedure is without a doubt the great chancellor of the University of Paris, Jean Gerson. An appropriate and necessary correction is provided in the excellent analysis of Gerson's ecclesiology by Guillaume H. M. Posthumus Meyjes. [11] Against de Vooght's allegation—which had a long pre-history—that Gerson is dependent upon Marsilius of Padua, Posthumus Meyjes documents clearly from the *Determinatio de iurisdictione spirituali* (dated by P.M. in early 1400) and from *De auferibilitate sponsi ab Ecclesia* of 1409 that Gerson explicitly and clearly rejected Marsilius' antipapal views (pp. 282f.). Even more important is the independence of Gerson from the laicizing ecclesiology of Occam, d'Ailly,

[10] S. Harrison Thomson (ed.), *Tractatus de Ecclesia* (Colorado, 1956), p. 70; cf. pp. 112f. The history of the discussion about the relation of *verus* to *vere* will have to be retraced to the extension of *fides* to *mores* (in the interpretation of Gratian's statement that the pope is not to be judged by anyone, *"nisi deprehendatur a fide devius"*) and the beginnings of the Investiture issue in the 11th century. Cf. footnote 22 and B. Tierney, *The Crisis of Church and State, 1050-1300* (Englewood Cliffs, N.J., 1964), pp. 33ff. Although not without precedent, Huss' radicalization may be seen in his transitions from prelate (*potestas iurisdictionis*) to priest (*potestas ordinis*): the power of the keys cannot be restricted to jurisdictional authority, but is rather the very basis for the sacerdotal power in the sacrament of penance.

[11] *Jean Gerson: zijn kerkpolitiek en ecclesiologie, avec une table des matières* ('s-Gravenhage, 1963); J. Bakhuizen van den Brink (ed.), *Kerkhistorische Studien* (in the series *Nederlands Archief voor Kerkgeschiedenis*).

Conrad von Gelnhaisen (d. 1390)[12] and Heinrich von Langen-
stein (d. 1397). Gerson rejects their thesis that *ius universitatis
in uno salvari potest,* illustrated by the figure of the Virgin Mary
who at the time of Christ's death stood fast while all disciples
fled.[13] Since Gerson, as a good disciple of Dionysius the Areo-
pagite, regards the Church as essentially hierarchical, the laity is
merely *ecclesia audiens* and therefore unable to provide continuity. The Church for him is essentially the hierarchy upon
whom the sacramental order is based. His sharp polemics against
the canon lawyers, and especially against the ultramontanist publicists, has often misled interpreters to regard him as a proponent
of a democratic church ideal.

In *De potestate ecclesiastica,* presented at the Council of Constance on February 6, 1417, Gerson charts a careful *via media*
between the absolutistic and spiritualistic doctrines of the Church.
He opposes the school of Aegidius Romanus, Augustinus Alvarez
Pelagius, Petrus de Palude (and, as one may add anachronis-

[12] The radical criticism of "the modern Church" that we find in such
late medieval preachers as Maillard (d. 1502), Geiler of Keisersberg (d.
1515) and Michel Menot (d. 1518) is traced by H. Riedlinger in his
history of exegesis of the Song of Songs back to the Parisian bishop
Gulielmus of Auvergne (d. 1249), later often copied, and quoted by
Conrad: *Die Makellosigkeit der Kirche in den Lateinischen Hohelied-
Kommentaren des Mittelalters* (Münster i. W., 1958), pp. 244ff., 357f.
One of these quotes expects from the leading clergy in the Church (*magi-
stratus Ecclesiae*) that combination of *verus* and *vere* which Huss is to
require from all clergymen; cf. *ibid.,* p. 359, footnote 5. For the point of
departure in canon law, cf. the careful discussion of the *Decretum* (Dist.
40, c. 6) and its interpretation by the influential decretist Huguccio (d.
1210) in B. Tierney, *Foundations of the Conciliar Theory* (Cambridge,
1955), pp. 59ff. We cannot show here in detail how many new perspectives Tierney's studies have opened up for the understanding of late medieval developments. We refer rather to A. Weiler, "Church Authority and
Government in the Middle Ages," in *Concilium 7: Historical Problems
of Church Renewal* (Glen Rock, N.J.: Paulist Press, 1965), pp. 123-36.
This article also discusses the works of Walter Ullman, Gaines Post and
M. J. Wilks. Cf. also K. Morrison, *The Two Kingdoms* (Princeton,
1964).

[13] J. Gerson, *op. cit.,* p. 219. It is here assigned to Conrad, but it can
be found with Occam, and perhaps has a common source in *Ecce Vicit
Leo* to Dist. 19, c. 9 of the *Decretum*; cf. B. Tierney, *op. cit.,* p. 44. In
Occam cf. *Dialogus* I, II, 25, photo reprint of the Lyon edition of 1494
by the Gregg Press, *Opera Plurime,* I (London, 1962).

tically, Silvester Prierias in his early writings against Luther), in their extension of the papal *plenitudo potestatis* to the point where the Church is absorbed by the pope (p. 230). In the closing section of Aegidius Romanus' *De ecclesiastica potestate,* it says indeed that the *potestas* of the pope is "spiritual, heavenly and divine, and without weight, number and measure".[14] We note the importance of this *sine pondere* for the ensuing late medieval debate about the indulgences in Aegidius' explanation that ". . . as for guilt and as for pain, in him [the sovereign pontiff] the burden is without weight, because in him there is so much power that it passes beyond all weight, that is, a question of weight of guilt or of weight of pain".[15]

After 1400 Gerson became increasingly convinced that such papal supremacy does not allow for a solution of the schism. While accepting the *plenitudo potestatis* as a papal prerogative, the *usus* of this power is to be regulated by the Council, since the *finis* of this power is the Church universal, represented by the Council. What Aegidius had assigned to the pope alone, Gerson ascribes to the whole hierarchy: over against Aegidius' *sine pondere, numero et mensura,* Gerson places the Council as "more vast in its amplitude or its extension . . . more vast because [it is] more abundant".[16] The author concludes that neither the *congregatio fidelium* of Marsilius nor the *ecclesia universalis* of Occam underlies this ecclesiology, in which the total hierarchy exceeds its parts (papacy, cardinalate, archepiscopate, episcopate and priesthood) without excluding any of these.

It is clear that Wyclif's and Huss' use of the distinction between *ecclesia* and *communio praedestinatorum* is completely alien to this ecclesiology and that de Vooght's thesis has to be reversed insofar as the attack of Gerson on Huss is not an effort to prove

[14] Vol. III, ch. 12 (ed. R. Scholz), p. 209. This excellent edition of 1929 is again available in photo reprint (Scientia Aalen, 1961): ". . . *spiritualis, celestis et divina, et est sine pondere, numero et mensura.*"

[15] *Ibid.,* ed. cit., pp. 208f.: ". . . *et quantum ad culpam ad penam, est in eo* [*summo pontifice*] *pondus sine pondere, quia est in eo tantum de posse, quod preponderat omni ponderi, sive sit pondus culpe, sive sit pondus pene.*"

[16] J. Gerson, *op. cit.,* p. 244 (ed. Dupin II, p. 248): ". . . *maior in amplitudine vel extensione . . . maior denique quia copiosior.*"

his doubtful orthodoxy,[17] but rather the consistent and organic application of his whole system of thought.

The chapter on "Church, Scripture and Tradition" is to a large extent a discussion of Gerson's hermeneutics. Here, even more clearly than in the formal treatment of the nature of the Church, the spiritualist position is rejected and sometimes explicitly called "Hussite". Against heretical subjectivism Gerson posits this thesis: "The meaning of scripture must be judged according to the determinations of the Church, inspired and governed by the Holy Spirit, and not according to free will or anyone's interpretation" [17a] (p. 262: ed. Dupin I, 3). The author is completely justified in concluding that dogma formulated in the past or still to be formulated in the future is regarded by Gerson in the proper literal sense. This literal sense does not arise out of scripture itself (*e mente auctorum*), but out of the Church (*e mente Auctoris*), led by the Spirit in all truth: "Ultimately Gerson does not follow through on his own basic principle that the literal sense of scripture is to be derived from scripture" (p. 264).

The effort made by Posthumus Meyjes to contrast Gerson's hierarchical vision of the Church with Occam's Church of laymen will have to be discussed in the light of Occam's own definition: "The universal Church also comprises the faithful Catholic princes and peoples, not only inasmuch as they live together this deficient life, but also inasmuch as they succeed each other." [18] The exceptional case of *Ecclesia in virgine continuata* is to be

[17] This is reaffirmed by de Vooght, "Jean Huss et ses juges," in *Das Konzil von Konstanz* (Festschrift Dr. Hermann Schäufele) (ed. A. Franzen and W. Müller) (Freiburg i. Br., 1964), p. 167: ". . . *la pensèe des d'Ailly et des Gerson, qui l'inspirèrent* [i.e., *la définition constancienne*], *est certainement héterodoxe.*" Among the unusually large number of important contributions to this Festschrift, we mention especially A. Franzen, "Zur Vorgeschichte des Konstanzer Konzils vom Ausbruch des Schismas bis zum Pisanum," *ibid.*, pp. 3-35, and in particular his section on Gerson, pp. 26f.

[17a] "*Sensus scripturae iudicandus est, prout Ecclesia Spiritu Sancto inspirata et gubernata, determinavit, et non ad cuiuslibet arbitrium vel interpretationem.*"

[18] *Contra Johannem*, XXII, p. 65; cf. *Dialogus* III, 4, 1, ch. 22, *ed. cit.*, p. 228: "*Ecclesia universalis, quae etiam fideles, non solum in hac vita simul degentes, sed sibimet succedentes, praelatos Catholicos comprehendit.*"

regarded as an illustration of an emergency situation (in Occam's words, *casualiter,* not *regulariter*) discussed by the decretists as an abstract possibility and quite realistically described by a number of commentators on the Song of Songs. The case of the Virgin Mary rather serves as the example of the basic thesis that "the universal Church cannot, not even for a moment, err from the truth either in faith or in morals. . . ." [19]

III

The conclusions of this fine study of Gerson are nevertheless supported by the last volume of George de Lagarde in his learned series *La Naissance de l'esprit laique au déclin du Moyen Age* which is especially concerned with Occam's ecclesiology.[20] From the outset it is clear that Occam has not found in de Lagarde a *defensor fidei (suae).* One does not have to read far (p. 11) to encounter as one of the themes running throughout this book that the multiform but rich and sound ecclesiology of the 12th and 13th centuries disintegrates under the pen of Occam. This sets the reviewer free to reverse the usual procedure and to give his final evaluation before presenting his thesis in more detail. When one wonders, after arriving at the last page of this impressive work, how it is possible that the texture of Occam's thought has not come through in the text even though every word in the text is well-documented, two answers suggest themselves.

In the first place, though a background sketch is offered in the first chapter, the immediate historical context of Occam's writings remains obscure.[21] The situation of the Western Church at

[19] *Dialogus* III, 4, 1, ch. 22, p. 228. Cf. the introduction to the edition of the *Breviloquium de principatu tyrannico* by R. Scholz, *Monumenta Germaniae Historica,* VIII (Stuttgart, 1952: photo reprint of 1944), pp. 26f.; P. Boehner, *Collected Articles on Ockham* (ed. E. Buytaert) (St. Bonaventure, 1958), pp. 450f.

[20] Vol. V, *Guillaume d'Ockham: Critique des structures ecclésiales* (Louvain-Paris, 1963).

[21] In Vol. IV of *Guillaume d'Ockham: Defense de l'empire* (Louvain, 1962), the historical background comes through much more clearly in

the time of the Avignon papacy, today generally presented in the darkest colors, determined Occam's every publication and made him a crisis theologian. Not Occam but the extent of the crisis forms the *discontinuum* with the two preceding centuries.

This leads to our second observation. The concluding words of Posthumus Meyjes about the evaluation of Gerson apply *suo modo* to research on Occam: "Those who are convinced that the [curialistic] canonists of the 13th and 14th century are normative will have little understanding and even less appreciation for Gerson" (p. 315). These words apply to the full extent to research on Occam, not so much in the sense that a good Occam scholar would necessarily have to despise the curialistic canonists and publicists, but so that a true Occam scholar has to do more than present—as de Lagarde certainly did—a well-documented report on the writings of the *inceptor venerabilis:* he will have to place Occam amidst the extremes shunned by him: the papal-triumphalistic ecclesiology of the curialists and the anti-institutional spiritualistic ecclesiology of late medieval spiritualism.

When the reader keeps these two concerns of Occam in mind, he will read de Lagarde's book with great profit. He will note the admission that Occam is not influenced by the Fraticelli and the Beguines,[22] and yet "on many points their critique of the ruling Church seemed to him worthy to be retained" (p. 29). The omitted complement to this observation, however, is equally im-

---

the total evaluation. In an exemplary fashion P. Classen has analyzed the thought of Gerhoh of Reichersberg (d. 1169) in constant reference to the historical events, reform needs, and schisms of his time: *Gerhoch von Reichersberg, Eine Biographie. Mit einem Anhang über die Quellen, ihre handschriftliche Überlieferung und ihre Chronologie* (Wiesbaden, 1960). For the study of the emergence of the conciliar idea and of the historical setting of the 12th-century decretists, this monograph is essential; cf. especially pp. 196ff., 316. The broad interest of the author in the history of Christian thought enriches this book, as, for example, the comparison of Gerhoh and Luther on the doctrine of the ubiquity of Christ on p. 242.

[22] The impact of the decisions of the Council of Vienna (1311-1312) on the "Sect of the Begards and the Beguines", its relation to the mendicant orders (especially in the years after 1318), and heterodoxy in these circles is carefully analyzed by E. Neumann, *Rheinisches Beginen—und Begarden Wesen* (Meisenheim Glau, 1959), with extensive bibliography.

portant, namely, that notwithstanding the divide between Occam and the curialists, their basic objections to sectarian spiritualism are retained.[23] In the concern to maintain this *via media* we have a more acceptable explanation (than in the traditional references to his nominalistic philosophy) why so little of the Franciscan spirituality, mysticism or prelude upon the *Devotio Moderna* comes through in Occam's polemical writings: it is the *spirituales* rather than the *termini* which form the restraining factors. On this second point the author is silent, and he can be silent because the sharp edges of the curialistic position, rejected by Occam, are not articulated (pp. 16, 134), and their proponents are usually subsumed under the general category of the "predecessors" (p. 48) from whom Occam deviates (p. 323). In a concluding section it is argued that this deviation is reflected if not dramatically hardened in the theology of the young Luther. Luther's pessimism and antirationalism are antitheses to Occamism, yet this movement, in which Luther was reared, continued to inform his style of thought and prepared the ground for the spread of the Reformation (pp. 297f.).

Insofar as it is clear that Occam, in contrast with Gerson, wants to emphasize the role of the laymen—women included— as forming not an appendix but pertaining to the essence of the Church, it is not inconceivable that in the period after Vatican Council II with its symbolic presence of *auditores* and *auditrices,* it could be more appreciated that the *inceptor venerabilis* has developed his ideas without assuming the sectarian contrast between the Spirit-guided lay Church and the visible-institutional Church of the *prelati.*

[23] Cf., for example, *Breviloquium,* II, ch. 4; *ed. cit.,* p. 21.

PART III
DO-C DOCUMENTATION
CONCILIUM

Office of the Executive Secretary
Nijmegen, Netherlands

James Hennesey, S.J./*New York, N.Y.*

A Comparative Study of American Participation in Vatican Councils I and II

Comparison of the role of the American Church in Vatican Council II with its role in the Council of 1869-1870 reveals remarkable similarities as well as notable differences. Paramount is the fact that the experience of Vatican Council I was primarily an episcopal experience, while that of Vatican Council II involved to a much greater degree the entire American Church body. Vatican Council I came and went, and it affected the American Church very little. Vatican Council II's effects have had, and will have, a profound influence in the future shaping of the Church in the United States. The reasons for the difference of effect are complex. They are to be found in the changed circumstances of the world, the nation and the Church.

In 1869 the United States was represented at Rome by 49 Council fathers. Their Church numbered 4,500,000 in a total national population of 40,000,000. A century later there were some 250 American fathers representing 45,000,000 American Catholics in a national population of 190,000,000. The United States in 1869 was on the fringe of the Western world, an isolated, third-rate power, recovering from the Civil War. In 1962 it was the international center of political and financial power, with its troops garrisoned from Berlin to Seoul. Memories of anti-Catholic nativism were vividly present to American Catholics in 1869. In 1960 the nation had elected its first Roman Catholic president. The country represented at Vatican Council I by a handful of bishops was represented at Vatican Council II by the second largest hierarchy in the Church.[1]

In the case of the bishops, there was a striking similarity between the conciliar experiences of 1869-1870 and 1962-1965. Archbishop Paul Hallinan, a historian of the American Church and an active participant in Vatican Council II, has found that in both instances the Americans "found their way, learned, matured and became articulate".[2] Other parallelisms exist in particular areas of concern, in a pastoral approach to problems, and even in the condescending appraisal made of the Americans. On December 12, 1869, the New York *Herald* editorialized that it was "a strange spectacle for the world at large—the bishops from the land that is foremost in all that material progress which is thought to be leading the nations . . . accepting the utmost the Church can require and leaving their brethren of the less progressive countries to assert the necessity for greater freedom of thought".[3] In 1965 an American historian commented: "In the preparatory stages of Vatican Council II, the unknown element at Rome was the part the North American bishops would play. With very few exceptions, they showed little interest, or perhaps understanding, of the issues involved. In Europe they were regarded as a hardworking, ingenuous, unsophisticated and theologically deficient lot." [4] Neither appraisal is accurate, but both are too frequently given uncritical acceptance.

There were differences between the American groups at the two Councils. Many of the fathers of 1869 were foreign-born immigrants to the United States. Thirty-five of the forty-nine

---

[1] For Vatican Council I, cf. J. Hennesey, *The First Council of the Vatican: The American Experience* (New York, 1963). The principal source used for Vatican Council II was F. Anderson (ed.), *Council Daybook, Vatican II* (3 vols.) (Washington, 1965-1966).

[2] P. Hallinan, "The American Bishops at the Vatican Councils," in *Catholic Historical Review* 51 (1965), p. 379.

[3] J. Hennesey, *op. cit.*, p. 51.

[4] B. Hill, "The North American Bishops and the Second Vatican Council," in *Colloquium* 4 (1965), p. 24.

had completed part of their seminary studies abroad—ten of them at Rome, another seven at St. Sulpice in Paris and the rest elsewhere in Europe.[5] By 1962 the percentage of Roman-trained bishops was higher, but many of the Americans had pursued seminary and graduate studies at home. A report to the Holy See in 1867 indicated that the diocesan chancery was almost unknown in America.[6] By 1962 critics would point to the chanceries as a major source of episcopal candidates and decry what they called the "chancery mentality".

In 1962, as in 1869, the problems facing the Church seemed to be largely of Europe's making. Reform of the Roman curia, the many-faceted scripture controversy, liturgical reform, ecumenism, the organizational structure of the Church, episcopal collegiality, the status of the laity, the nature of ecclesiastical authority—all of these and other areas hotly debated in Europe were not burning issues in America, at least not on the surface. A century ago there was no profound American interest in the temporal power of the pope, the need to define infallibility or the challenge of liberalism, rationalism and anti-clericalism. In 1869-1870 Americans soon divided on the central issue of the Council, that of papal infallibility. To a much greater extent all that was involved in the *aggiornamento* found its way into the American Catholic consciousness of the 1960s with a startling suddenness, as problems which had been festering under the surface burst out under the pressure of the Council.

One factor which contributed to make the impact of Vatican Council II broader and deeper than that of Vatican Council I was the strange chemistry effected by the combined influence of Pope John XXIII and President John F. Kennedy, two men so very different, but each of whom responded to deeply felt needs of the age. A second factor was the rapid circulation of ideas and the growing community of basic interests which have been a phenomenon of the post-World War II era. In 1869 the problems facing the Council were of ecclesiastical and European

[5] J. Code, *Dictionary of the American Hierarchy* (New York, 1940).
[6] Mansi 49, 265.

political interest. The arguments pro and con were known in the United States, but hardly impressed those who were not professional churchmen as of vital importance. In the years prior to Vatican Council II the thought of scholars like Rahner, de Lubac, Congar and others had begun to exercise a profound effect on the thinking of American Catholic intellectuals. Only a spark was needed, and the Council provided it. The works and lectures of Hans Küng and others mediated this consciousness more widely. On the domestic scene names like Murray, Weigel and Diekmann emerged from the technical theological journals and their ideas became known to increasingly broader circles.

The great development during the past century of media of communication contributed mightily to the impact of Vatican Council II on the American scene. In the 1860s the unique medium of communication was the newspaper. The American secular press was almost uniformly hostile to the Council, the papacy, and everything connected with them.[7] Press, television, radio and the newspapers gave an entirely different picture of the situation in Rome during the Council just finished. By and large, the reporters were sympathetic, knowledgeable, comprehensive and penetrating. An American (or Americans) named Xavier Rynne helped to break the silence barrier originally intended to surround the conciliar proceedings, and the United States Bishops' Press Panel provided valuable service to the reporters and, through them, to the world.

In the inner workings of the Council the United States was represented by a fair sampling of members and consultors on the preparatory commissions, by a good number of bishops on the conciliar commissions, and by *periti* who contributed in varying degrees to the Council's work. All of this was in considerable contrast to the situation at Vatican Council I where only a single American participated in preparation of the agenda and where but six bishops from the United States served on the Council's commissions.[8] All of these factors—the mood of the

[7] J. Beiser, *American Secular Newspapers and the Vatican Council* (Washington, 1942).

[8] J. Hennesey, "James A. Corcoran's Mission to Rome: 1868-1869,"

Johannine era, the growing international consciousness of basic interests, the wider circulation and assimilation of theological ideas, the favorable and informative attitude of communications media and the greater involvement of the American Church in the Council—reacted upon a more sophisticated, better educated, more intellectually aware Catholic community in the United States to make Vatican Council II in a very special sense a Council of the whole Church and not just of its hierarchical leaders.

One of the facts most disconcerting to the American church historian is the lack of a historical sense, or indeed the lack of any real interest in developing a historical sense, which he finds among his contemporaries. Studying the two Vatican Councils, he is struck by the factors in the American conciliar experience that have remained constant, but he realizes that this continuity has very little meaning in terms of a theological development conditioned by the American scene. The Church in the United States is always beginning anew, frequently borrowing insights from elsewhere which it might find simply by looking into its own heritage. An example of this is the question of episcopal collegiality.

Nowhere in the 19th-century Western Church did the conciliar and collegial tradition take deeper root than it did in the United States. The American expression of that tradition began with the three General Chapters of the Clergy held in Maryland between 1783 and 1789. These were followed by the Baltimore Diocesan Synod of 1791, the Bishops' Meeting of 1810, the seven Provincial Councils of Baltimore between 1829 and 1849, and the two Plenary Councils of Baltimore in 1852 and 1866. In each case the assembly represented the entire American Church.[9] Writing in 1839, the foremost contemporary American theologian, Francis P. Kenrick, penned an explicit statement of the existence of the *collegium episcopale* and of its role vis-à-vis the

in *Catholic Historical Review* 48 (1962), pp. 157-81; *idem, The First Council of the Vatican, op. cit.,* pp. 48-9.

[9] P. Guilday, *A History of the Councils of Baltimore: 1791-1884* (New York, 1932).

pope. In the Roman meetings which preceded the 1854 definition of the immaculate conception, Bishop Michael O'Connor,
Roman-trained like Kenrick, asked explicitly that the definition
be made with the consent of the bishops.[10] The Baltimore Plenary
Council of 1866 reaffirmed the existence and prerogatives of
the episcopal college as successor to the apostles.[11] At Vatican
Council I a primary reason for American opposition to the definition of infallibility was the fact that the bishops could not see
how the proposed text safeguarded the episcopal position.[12] In
the related area of papal primacy, it was Archbishop Spalding
of Baltimore who secured inclusion in the text of a statement to
the effect that ordinary and immediate papal jurisdiction did not
conflict with local episcopal jurisdiction.[13]

The American bishops met once more in council in 1884, and
since that time there have been regular meetings, first of the
metropolitans and then, since World War I, of the entire hierarchy. No jurisdiction is involved in these meetings, and it was
their influence, rather than the earlier and longer conciliar tradition, which shaped the thinking of the bishops of Vatican Council
II.[14] Cardinal Spellman found the jurisdictional implications of
collegiality to be at variance with what he had learned in the
seminary.[15] Other Americans were more favorably disposed, but
even a progressive like Cardinal Meyer moved gingerly and
was hesitant about the intrusion of national episcopal jurisdiction
into the diocesan regime.[16]

One strong advocate of the idea of collegiality was Cardinal
Ritter, but his intervention made no reference to the strong American tradition on the point.[17] Only the intervention of Cardinal Shehan of Baltimore seemed to echo the earlier thought

[10] J. Hennesey, "Prelude to Vatican I: American Bishops and the Definition of the Immaculate Conception," in *Theol. Stud.* 25 (1964), pp.
413, 418; *idem, The First Council of the Vatican, op. cit.,* pp. 205-6.

[11] *Coll. Lacen.* 3, 413.

[12] J. Hennesey, *The First Council of the Vatican, op. cit.,* p. 312.

[13] *Ibid.,* p. 222.

[14] F. Anderson, *op. cit.,* I, pp. 231-2, 256.

[15] *Ibid.,* p. 251.

[16] *Ibid.,* pp. 168, 256-7.

[17] *Ibid.*

of the American Church, and specifically of his predecessor Martin Spalding, when he called for a clarification which would make it plain that there was no incompatibility between the position of the bishops and that of the pope.[18] But it must be admitted that the American bishops of Vatican Council II did not bring to bear the contribution which they might have made to the discussion on collegiality from the experience of the Church in the United States.

In another area of discussion, that of the interrelation of hierarchy, clergy and laity, the American contribution at Vatican Council II surpassed that at Vatican Council I. During Vatican Council I there was considerable agitation in the United States on behalf of parish priests, who were termed the "second order of the hierarchy". Although the agitation resulted in one bishop being forced to resign his See, the American hierarchy in the main withstood the challenge.[19] The bishop of a century ago was supreme in his diocese. Involvement of the laity in Church affairs was also under a cloud. While strong-minded editors like James A. MacMaster of the *Freeman's Journal* did not hesitate to dispense advice on any and every ecclesiastical matter, the problem of lay trusteeism in the control of property was too recent to make the bishops amenable to ideas of greater lay involvement in Church business. In the sessions of 1964 and 1965, however, several of the Americans spoke their mind forthrightly. Cardinal Shehan called for greater understanding of the participation of priests and bishops in the one priesthood.[20] Auxiliary Bishop Stephen A. Leven of San Antonio spoke out on behalf of curates, and he also delivered a powerful plea for real dialogue between hierarchy and laity.[21] In the latter connec-

---

[18] *Ibid.*, pp. 177-8.

[19] The leader of the campaign for the "second order of the hierarchy" was Rev. Eugene M. O'Callaghan of Cleveland. The story of the movement is yet to be told. Fr. O'Callaghan represented the *Freeman's Journal* in Rome during the Council. Cf. J. Hennesey, *The First Council of the Vatican, op. cit.*, p. 118.

[20] *Council Digest* 4 (Oct. 16, 1965). This publication was prepared for the use of the American bishops by the Rome office of the N.C.W.C.

[21] F. Anderson, *op. cit.*, II, pp. 115-6.

tion he recalled the diocesan constitution set up in the early 19th century by Bishop John England of Charleston and suggested it as a model for creation of diocesan and parish senates.[22] Cardinal Ritter strongly opposed the clerical tone of the schema on the lay apostolate and called for a more careful theological grounding which would express the reality of the laity's role in the Church.[23] Despite admitted difficulties in the area of clerical-lay relationships, the American bishops of Vatican Council II were able to speak from an experience of better rapport than is found in many places, and they did so.

The Americans at both Councils were sometimes dismissed as "pragmatists". Archbishop Hallinan has pointed out that the word "pragmatic" can, with proper reservations, be translated "pastoral".[24] Bishop Verot of Savannah was one such American pragmatist at Vatican Council I. His call for rapprochement between the Church and modern science would have fitted in well at Vatican Council II.[25] Cardinal Meyer and Cardinal Shehan provided theoretical support for the American approach by pointing to the need for compenetration between the world and the Church, since the world itself, and not only man, is the proper object of redemption, and since in the real order the natural and the supernatural are complementary in the same subject.[26] Bishop Leven brought the discussion on ecumenism into perspective by reminding the fathers that he and his colleagues spoke from experience of living with non-Catholics and of promoting a program of religious education in a pluralist society.[27] His intervention was reminiscent of those of many Americans a century ago who kept reminding the fathers of Vatican Council I of the realities of the world in which they lived. In emotionally charged areas such as nuclear disarmament

[22] *Ibid.*, p. 118.

[23] *Ibid.*, p. 112.

[24] P. Hallinan, *op. cit.*, p. 381.

[25] M. Gannon, *Rebel Bishop* (Milwaukee, 1964); this is the standard biography of Verot.

[26] F. Anderson, *op. cit.*, II, pp. 163-4; *Council Digest* (Sept. 23, 1965), pp. 3-4.

[27] F. Anderson, *op. cit.*, I, p. 305.

and family limitation American bishops in 1965 did not hesitate to take stands which they felt were realistic, if not necessarily popular.[28]

Ecumenism was one area in which the American practical approach won out over initial reserve. Interfaith association was the exception, rather than the rule, in the pre-Vatican Council II American Church, but it has won wide acceptance in consequence of the Council's decree. Here again a developing American position had been lost sight of between the two Councils. In 1869-1870 many of the American interventions reflected the experience of living in a pluralist society. Bishops Elder and Whelan stressed the necessity of careful use of scripture, and Bishops Amat and Lynch emphasized the goodwill and religious sincerity of their Protestant compatriots.[29] The waves of immigration which subsequently isolated the Catholic Church and its concerns from the nation, and the fear complex created half a century or more ago by the Americanist and Modernist crises halted for a time the movement in American Catholicism toward what we call today ecumenism, but it has begun again in the wake of Vatican Council II.

The question of liturgical reform presents another fascinating phenomenon. Five years ago even the most ardent American enthusiast would not have predicted the revolution in liturgical worship that has taken place. But at the very first session of the Council Archbishop Hallinan took the lead in marshaling the American forces in favor of it. The changes have not come about without the opposition of both clerical and lay sources, but they have come about. The question was not on the agenda of Vatican Council I, but it is well to record the fact that in 1787 John Carroll, three years later to become the first American bishop, wrote that introduction of a vernacular liturgy was "essential to the service of God and the benefit of mankind".[30] The *Declaration on the Relation of the Church to Non-Christian*

[28] F. Anderson, *op. cit.*, II, pp. 247-8.
[29] J. Hennesey, *The First Council of the Vatican, op. cit.*, pp. 134-42.
[30] J. T. Ellis, *Perspectives in American Catholicism* (Benedictine Studies, 5) (Baltimore, 1963), p. 129.

Religions was another new item at Vatican Council II and it is noteworthy that American support for it was overwhelming.

The *Declaration on Religious Freedom* has been described as *the* American issue of Vatican Council II.[31] Had there been time, it might also have been the American issue of Vatican Council I. In the preparatory commission of that Council, the lone American fought hard to prevent canonization of the principle of union of Church and State.[32] In the Council itself Archbishop Purcell was prepared to declare boldly that perfect liberty for all denominations was infinitely better for the Catholic religion than that it be the special object of the State's patronage and protection.[33] The issue never came before Vatican Council I, but under the leadership of Cardinal Spellman the American bishops were strongly influential in bringing it to the attention of the fathers of Vatican Council II. Once the topic had come to the floor a whole succession of Americans argued the theoretical, ecumenical and pastoral reasons for adoption of the Declaration.[34] It is generally recognized that one of the principal architects of the Council's statement on the subject was the American Jesuit John Courtney Murray. The speech which Archbishop Purcell prepared for delivery in 1870 relied heavily on pastoral considerations. The American position presented at Vatican Council II remained conscious of these. It also provided philosophical, theological and juridical arguments which helped to convince the fathers of the need for a clear and unambiguous statement on the subject.

The American experience at the two Vatican Councils was not uniform. Too much had happened in the intervening century for that. There were similarities, perhaps the most pronounced of

---

[31] J. C. Murray, "Thoughts in Midstream," in *Vatican II* (New York, 1964), pp. 43-4.

[32] J. Hennesey, "James A. Corcoran's Mission to Rome: 1868-1869," in *Catholic Historical Review,* 48 (1962), pp. 164-5, 169-71.

[33] J. Hennesey, *The First Council of the Vatican, op. cit.,* pp. 132-3.

[34] Among the more significant American interventions were those of Cardinals Shehan, Cushing, Meyer and Ritter, Bishop Primeau and Archbishop Alter, all in the third session, and of Cardinals Cushing, Ritter and Shehan and Archbishop Hallinan during the fourth session.

which was the continued pastoral emphasis on the part of the bishops. Americans, with some exceptions, have not yet become theoreticians, but they did contribute at both Councils an awareness of the modern world and of the needs of the apostolate. The effects of Vatican Council II in the American Church have yet to be seen. The signs are that there will be a more demanding and articulate laity, a modification of structural rigidity and a greater reflex consciousness of the meaning and the demands of Catholic faith. Vatican Council II's impact on Catholic and non-Catholic alike has been vastly greater than that of its predecessor. The Church in the United States has turned a corner and it will not turn back. In some quarters there is a mood of disparagement of the past and its accomplishments. Hopefully a greater knowledge of the real facts of that past will serve to fortify and strengthen and give courage to American Catholics as they move into the latest post-conciliar era in the history of the Church.

Charles Moeller/*Louvain, Belgium*

Projected Ecumenical Institute at Jerusalem

I

FROM ROME TO JERUSALEM

1. *A Brief History*

Addressing the Pope at an audience for the observers during the second session of Vatican Council II, Professor Skydsgaard of the faculty of Lutheran theology in Copenhagen emphasized the value of theological research carried out on an ecumenical basis. Among other things, he mentioned the theme of salvation history which the researches of Oscar Cullmann have brought into prominence. According to Skydsgaard, this theme, which the Eastern tradition calls "salvation economy", could be an excellent common meeting ground for research. In his reply, Pope Paul VI indicated great interest in such an idea.

In the course of his pilgrimage to the Holy Land, Paul VI considered giving concrete effect to this suggestion in the shape of an ecumenical research institute at Jerusalem, for this city clearly manifests the essential bond between the Church and Jesus Christ which the Pope was to place at the heart of his encyclical *Ecclesiam suam*.[1]

In April, 1964, the Pope instructed Fr. Hesburgh, C.S.C.,

---

[1] *De Rome à Jérusalem, itinéraire théologique de Vatican II* by B. Lambert (Paris, 1964), stresses the theological significance of the pope's pilgrimage.

President of the International Federation of Catholic Universities and Rector of the University of Notre Dame, Notre Dame, Ind., to take the necessary steps for setting up an institute to be run as a truly ecumenical university. A provisional commission (within which an executive committee was formed) started work immediately. The sessions of Vatican Council II, as well as many journeys to such countries as Jordan, Lebanon, Egypt, Greece, Switzerland, England, Japan and North and South America, enabled the commission to achieve its aim to remain in continual contact with the separated brethren.

The preparations resulted in the formation of the first Academic Committee of the Institute at the Rockefeller Foundation, Bellagio, November 26-28, 1965. On December 15 the communiqué which follows was ready for release to the press.

2. The Bellagio Communiqué

"A group of theologians, Roman Catholic, Orthodox (Chalcedonian and non-Chalcedonian), Protestant and Anglican, gathered together at Villa Serbelloni (conference center of the Rockefeller Foundation) situated at Bellagio on Lake Como in Italy, have set themselves up as the Academic Committee of an Ecumenical Institute for theological research which is to be founded at Jerusalem, Jordan. This step was taken in response to an invitation from the International Federation of Catholic Universities, to which Pope Paul VI had entrusted the task of taking the initiative in this matter. In the course of recent ecumenical gatherings, the wish had been expressed for a program of common theological research, the principal theme of which would be the redeeming action of God in history and the significance of this fact for men of today. The Institute is planned in order to put this idea into effect.

"The members of the Academic Committee have studied the academic, administrative and financial problems which the establishment of the Ecumenical Institute is likely to raise, as well as the questions of program and staff. It has been agreed that the program should have a full university character. The first and main purpose of the Institute will be to provide qualified research workers and students who already have a degree in theology with the means to carry out research on an ecumenical basis. It is hoped that later the Institute will become a center from which— by means of individual studies, seminars and conferences—an ecumenical vision will spread among clergy and laity. The Academic Committee also intends that the study program should be carried on in an atmosphere of prayer and worship.

"The Institute is to be fully ecumenical in both spirit and structure. The members of the Academic Committee have been invited to collaborate in the affairs of the Institute because of their experience in ecumenism, as well as their university qualifications. The Committee will take on full responsibility for directing the academic side of the Institute." [2]

[2] The following members of the Academic Committee were present at the Bellagio meetings: Dr. Robert McAfee Brown (Presbyterian United Church, U.S.A.), Stanford University, California; Rev. Walter J. Burghardt, S.J. (Roman Catholic), Woodstock College, Maryland; Principal J. Russell Chandran (Church of South India), United Theological College (University of Serampore), Bangalore, India; Professor Panayotis Christou (Orthodox), Vice-Rector, University of Thessalonica, Greece; Rev. Yves Congar, O.P. (Roman Catholic), Strasbourg, France; Professor Oscar Cullmann (Lutheran Church), Universities of Basel and Paris, Basel, Switzerland; Dr. Eugene Fairweather (Anglican), Faculty of Theology, Trinity College, University of Toronto, Canada; Rev. Jean Feiner (Roman Catholic), Seminary of St. Luzi, Coire, Switzerland; Very Rev. Georges Florovsky (Orthodox), Department of Religion, Princeton University, Princeton, New Jersey; Rev. Theodore Hesburgh, C.S.C. (Roman Catholic), President of the International Federation of Catholic Universities; Dr. K. C. Joseph (Indian Orthodox Church), Dean, Theological College of the Holy Trinity of the Ethiopian Orthodox Church, Addis Ababa, Ethiopia; Dr. John N. D. Kelly (Anglican), Principal of St. Edmund Hall, Oxford University, England; Professor Arthur C. McGill (United Church of Christ), Department of Religion, Princeton University, Princeton, New Jersey; Rev. Jorge E. Medina (Roman Catholic), Dean of the Faculty of Theology, Catholic University of Chile, Santiago, Chile; Professor Paul Minear (United Church, U.S.A.), Theological School, Yale University, New Haven, Connecticut; Rev. Charles O. Moeller (Roman Catholic), Professor, University of Louvain, Belgium; Dr. Albert Outler (Methodist Church, U.S.A.), Perkins School of Theology, Methodist University of the South, Dallas, Texas; Dean Howard Root (Anglican), Emmanuel College, Cambridge University, England; H.E. Msgr. Karekin Sarkissian (non-Chalcedonian Orthodox), Rector, Faculty of Armenian Theology, Antelias, Lebanon; Professor Rudolf Schnackenburg (Roman

II

STRUCTURE AND FUNCTION OF THE INSTITUTE

The Academic Committee which will direct the Institute will be composed of professors belonging to different Christian Churches and Confessions. The members of this Committee must not exceed thirty in number.

The Committee will have the task of appointing the permanent staff of the Jerusalem Institute. This staff, consisting of five to seven members of different Christian Churches and Confessions, will be in charge of the Institute.

It is also planned to form a Board of Governors, composed not of academics but of well-known churchmen. The purpose of this board will be to show that the work of the Institute is being carried on with the agreement and support of the Churches.

There will be three levels of work at the Institute:

1. First, and most important, there will be research on a purely scientific level. One example that could be given is the possibility of examining the most ancient versions of the text of the bible, not in order to establish the text, but to see how, at the beginning of the Church's history, the mentality of different local Churches reacted to the preaching of the Word of God. Another good example is the possibility of studying the history of the first Christian theological schools: Syrian, Greek, Armenian, Latin,

---

Catholic), Professor, Faculty of Catholic Theology, Würzburg University, Germany; Professor Joseph Sittler (Lutheran Church, U.S.A.), Faculty of Theology, University of Chicago, Illinois.

Because of unforeseen circumstances, the following were unable to take part in the meeting: Rev. Pierre Benoit, O.P. (Roman Catholic), Rector, Ecole Biblique, Jerusalem, Jordan; Professor Carnic (Orthodox), Belgrade, Yugoslavia; H.E. Msgr. Chrysostome Constantinidis (Orthodox), Metropolitan of Myra, Professor at Khalci, Istanbul, Turkey; Professor Küppers (Old Catholic), Bonn Seminary, Germany; Rev. Raymond Pannikar (Roman Catholic), Varanasi, India; Professor Edmund Schlink (Lutheran Church), Professor, Faculty of Theology, Heidelberg University, Germany; Professor Markos Siotis (Orthodox), Professor at the Faculty of Theology, University of Athens, Greece. In case of absence, Professor Skydsgaard will take the place of Professor Schlink.

Other nominations to the Academic Committee will be announced later.

etc. This research work will be carried on by professors and by graduate students who wish to prepare a thesis or to go on to some specialized work or research after their thesis, under the direction of professors expert in that field.

2. On a second level, one foresees the possibility of training courses of two or three months for theologians or seminary professors. The aim of these courses would be to help them to orient their studies and theological instruction more toward the biblical and patristic perspective of salvation history, and to impart to them the fruits of the research work carried out in the Institute.

3. A third possible level might be that of broader and more popular courses designed for pastors, priests, religious or lay theologians already possessing sufficient theological training. The aim of these sessions would be to aid the participants to deepen their biblical and patristic knowledge.

III

POSSIBLE THEOLOGICAL PROGRAM OF THE INSTITUTE

1. *Aims of the Institute*

Some have suggested as a theme: "Christian research in face of the problems of the modern world."

The object of the research must afford a wide scope and bear on points which have a common interest for all Christians, bringing them together in a common theological task. It must help them to become aware of the universality of God's Word which is addressed to all men. The principal object of research therefore seems to be the significance of the "economy" of salvation for all humanity, touching on every dimension of the history of the human race. In this way, theologians of all the Christian Churches will be able to give a common witness to the world of their hope of salvation.

Therefore, there will be research into how, for example, the different Christian traditions resemble each other and how they differ from the point of view of the history or "economy" of salvation which is rooted in the biblical soil. In view of Christian reunion, the *unity* contained within the multiplicity of Christian traditions must be rediscovered. The *universality* of the Word of God must also be rediscovered with respect to Judaism, Islam, the great non-Christian religions and the non-believing world.

To achieve this, a twofold form of activity seems necessary: on the one hand, there must be a return to the sources; on the other, dialogue becomes a necessity.

(a) *Return to the Sources.* It is important to rediscover the continuity with the past. Jerusalem is a meeting-place of Eastern and Western traditions; moreover, the biblical origin shared by all Christians exercises a reconciling influence upon the thoughts and feelings of the separated brethren. The research must go back beyond philosophical and theological developments as well as beyond cultural and canonical applications. At the same time, this raises a problem of central importance: namely, the critique of theological knowledge. We need to compile a history of theological method, tracing the course of the great turning points which it has known. There are some very serious problems here for research workers to tackle.

(b) *Dialogue.* We must find out how to rediscover the freshness and originality which touches on the essential element in the history of salvation. The more we succeed in this, the more will we show how open the "economy" of salvation is to new cultures, as, for example, that of Africa which is so akin in certain respects to the biblical setting.

2. *Possible Object of Research*

(a) *Return to the Sources and Unity.* The following are possible subjects for study (I have already mentioned some of them):

(1) The history of the different versions of scripture, with the aim not of establishing the text but of discovering from it the way in which different Christian Churches have reacted to the Word of God.

(2) The history of the formation of the first theological traditions as they were developed around the revealed deposit of faith which is fundamentally biblical. Here research workers, keeping within the bounds of the Christian East, should examine the role of the Stoic, neo-Platonist and Aristotelian philosophies, selecting concrete examples. It would thus be possible to bring out the essential points of the three great streams of theological tradition: the Syrian (or Semitic), the Byzantine and the Western.

Within these same bounds there could be research into the history of the ancient Churches: for example, the Nestorians and Monophysites, whether Syrian, Coptic or Armenian.

(3) The history of the formation of liturgical traditions (in this sphere one could recover some of the elements of an oral tradition going back to the apostolic period: for example, in the texts of the anaphoras which tell of the Last Supper) and also of spiritual, mystical and canonical traditions.

These suggestions are not exhaustive. It is important to look for research perspectives which interest Christians of the reformed tradition. By studying these ancient periods, it is possible to rediscover the very diverse cultures to which the primitive Church adapted itself. This is of great interest in the present situation.

(b) *Dialogue and Universality*. Under this heading one might study the following, some of which, again, have already been mentioned:

(1) *Vis-à-vis the Christian world:* the history of theological method and its great turning points ("Hellenization", Scholasticism, the Reformation and Counter-Reformation, modern Christianity); the present situation of Christian theologies in the great Christian Churches represented in the East by comparison of theological manuals and problems of evangelism.

(2) *Vis-à-vis the Jewish religion:* the history of Jewish Christianity, ancient and modern; the history of Jewish tradition in the ancient East (for example, its influence on certain texts of St. John Chrysostom); the present situation of religious Judaism.

(3) *Vis-à-vis Islam:* the history of the first encounters between Islam and Christianity (apologetic writings in languages such as

Syriac, Arabic, etc.); study of the Arab tradition in its natural environment in Jerusalem, in Hebron and in other places in the East; the position of Islam in the world today.

(4) *Vis-à-vis the nations of Africa and Asia:* the history of the apostolic expansion of the Syrian Churches toward Persia, India and China; study of the possibilities of rooting Christianity in the cultures of Asia and Africa, using dialogue and a return to the biblical sources in the context of salvation history; a thorough study of Christian responsibility toward the world.

(5) *Vis-à-vis "secularism"* (i.e., what is sometimes called "Christian atheism" as well as all those movements which have a "religious" character but which distrust theology and the Churches): themes like those of the *Constitution on the Church in the Modern World* could be made the object of shared research.[3]

IV

CONCLUSION

At the end of the first two years spent in preparing for the Institute (April 1964 to April 1966), what has emerged more clearly than anything else is the significant fact that the ecumenical character of the Institute does not depend on the object chosen for research, but rather on the work which is done together, dealing with problems which interest all Christians: the doctrine of man, the significance of the idea of God (and the meaning of atheism), christology (the risen Christ and history) and eschatology. This is what is clearly apparent in the theme of salvation.

Further, it appears essential to approach the research simultaneously from two angles: the one, biblical, patristic, conciliar,

[3] The present address of the secretariat of the Institute is: c/o Secrétariat pour l'unité, Via dell' Erba, 1, Rome. (Write to P. Duprey.) Information can also be obtained from: Rev. Theodore Hesburgh, President, University of Notre Dame, Notre Dame, Indiana, U.S.A.

liturgical and historical; the other, phenomenological, analytic and reflective, starting from modern problems.

Jerusalem is the holy city of all Christians. The rebirth in space and time, of which we are reminded by every stone and event in this place of holiness and sorrow, will make clearer the universality of the hope of salvation in the face of the great non-Christian religions and before the watchful eyes of the world. This by no means will be in spite of the Jerusalem setting, but because of it. "If I forget thee, O Jerusalem. . . .": the psalm is truer and more prophetic than ever.

Francis Dvornik/*Washington, D.C.*

Preambles to the Schism of Michael Cerularius

The break between the Roman and Eastern Churches in 1054 did not come unexpectedly. The full responsibility for this unfortunate happening cannot be laid only at the feet of the haughty Patriarch of Constantinople, Michael Cerularius.[1] The figures of the Patriarch and of Cardinal Humbert appeared only at the end of a long list of Eastern and Western spiritual leaders and statesmen who laid the ground for the estrangement which ended in the condemnation of Michael Cerularius by Cardinal Humbert. Nor can we consider these leaders as always personally responsible for its development.

Political ideology and political events influenced this estrangement more than dogma. Even the last act of this tragic drama had a more political than religious background. The political philosophy of the early Christians was an adaptation of the Hellenistic system to Christian belief. The Hellenistic king was deprived of his divine character, but he was regarded as chosen by God to be his representative on earth. Constantine the Great (306-337) accepted this adaptation and regarded the care for the Church and protection of the true religion as the main part of his imperial duties.[2] The Roman Empire was the *oikumene,* the only part of

---

[1] Cf. A. Michel, *Humbert und Kerullarios—Duellen und Studien zum Schisma des XI. Jahrhunderts,* I-II (Paderborn, 1925, 1930).

[2] For details, cf. F. Dvornik, *Early Christian and Byzantine Political Philosophy: Origins and Background* (Dumbarton Oaks Studies, 9) (Dumbarton Oaks: Washington, D.C., 1966).

the world known at that time, and the Church adapted its own organization to the political divisions of the Empire. Rome remained its base, even when the residence of the emperor was transferred to Constantinople. The Byzantines called themselves not Greeks but Romans. The papacy accepted the political supremacy of the emperor and often sanctioned even his interventions in religious affairs.

As long as the idea of one emperor appointed by God and of one Empire was generally accepted, the relations between Rome and Constantinople were normal. Not even the tempests raised by the christological disputes could disrupt these relations. The schism provoked by the adherence of Patriarch Acacius (472-489) to monophysitism accepting the existence of only one nature in the incarnate Word was ended by Justinian (527-565) in favor of Pope Hormisdas (519-523). Confirming the privileged position of Rome in the Empire, Justinian declared: "Old Rome has the honor of being the mother of law and none will doubt that she is the head of the supreme pontificate." He called Rome "the head of all holy Churches" and asserted that he could not tolerate "that anything concerning the ecclesiastical order should be settled independently of his Holiness (the pope), since he is the head of all the sacred priests of God".[3]

However, Justinian's renovation of the Roman Empire lasted only a short time. The foundation of a new Germanic kingdom in northern Italy by Lombard invaders raised unforeseen obstacles in the improvement of good relations between Rome and Constantinople. The progress of the Lombards toward Rome was becoming increasingly menacing. Gregory the Great (590-604) defended Rome, remaining loyal to the emperor, although he was unable to help Gregory in the defense of Italy. Emperor Phocas confirmed the privileged position of Rome in the Empire (607) and the incidents provoked by the monotheletistic heresy were forgotten when the Sixth Ecumenical Council (680-681) had

---

[3] F. Dvornik, *Byzance et la Primauté Romaine* (Unam Sanctam, 49) (Paris, 1964), pp. 61ff.: Eng. tr.: *Byzantium and the Roman Primacy* (Fordham University Press: New York, 1966).

approved the dogmatic missives of Pope Agatho on the two wills in Christ.

The popes elected by the Roman clergy continued to inform the representatives of the emperor at Ravenna of their election, asking the emperor's confirmation.[4] In 710 Pope Constantine was received in Constantinople with great respect by the emperor and the people of the capital. Justinian II confirmed anew the Roman primacy in ecclesiastical matters as had Justinian I and Phocas.[5]

The ambitions of the Lombard King Aistulf provoked a new crisis. In 751 he took Ravenna and threatened to annex Rome. Zachary, the last pope who had announced his election to Emperor Constantine V and asked for its confirmation, was unable to stop the Lombard advance. By giving his moral sanction to the elevation of Pippin to the Frankish throne, he put the new dynasty into obligation to Rome. This was exploited by his successor, Stephen II (752-757).

The emperor, unable to provide troops for the protection of Rome, sent the pope with his envoy to Aistulf with the request to stop the menace to Rome and to restore Ravenna to the Empire. When the king had refused the pope's request, Stephen II went to Pippin asking for help. After defeating Aistulf, Pippin donated the exarchate of Ravenna and the duchy of Rome to the pope.[6] But this was not yet the end of the old tradition that there was only one emperor, residing in Constantinople. Pippin remained in good rapport with the emperor, and in the territory given by him to the pope the authority of the emperor continued to be recognized at least outwardly.

Not even the storm provoked by the iconoclastic emperors brought an end to the peaceful relations between Rome and Constantinople. Good relations were restored on the occasion of the Seventh Ecumenical Council (787), and Empress Irene

[4] The diplomatic formulas are preserved in *Liber Diurnus Romanorum Pontificum* (ed. H. Foerster) (Bern, 1958).

[5] *Liber Pontificalis,* I (ed. L. Duchesne) (Paris, 1886), p. 316.

[6] For details, cf. A. Fliche and V. Martin, *Histoire de l'Eglise,* V-VI (Paris, 1947).

called the pope in her letter the "truly first priest, who presides instead of the holy and all-praised apostle Peter and in his chair".[7]

The fateful break occurred in the reign of Pope Leo III (795-816). Opposed by the Roman aristocracy and needing the support of an emperor, the pope threw himself completely into the arms of Pippin's successor, Charlemagne, who had made a definite end to the Lombard kingdom, and he proclaimed him emperor of the Romans on Christmas night in the year 800. Probably he regarded the imperial throne in Constantinople as vacant when Constantine VI had been deposed by his mother Irene. He also might have been influenced by the famous falsification—the *Donatio Constantini*—according to which Constantine the Great, before moving to Constantinople, had bestowed on the pope all imperial possessions in Italy. This falsification was probably fabricated by some Roman clerics, anxious to give to Pippin's donation a more legal base, because they were conscious that only the Emperor of Constantinople could have made such a disposition.

In the eyes of the Byzantines such an act was regarded as treachery and insurrection against the lawful Roman emperor. Charlemagne was well aware of this and tried to legalize the papal action by a marriage with Empress Irene. Her deposition by Nicephorus I (811-813) ended this compromise. The war initiated by Nicephorus against the usurper ended with Charlemagne's victory, and Charlemagne was greeted by Byzantine envoys as *basileus*—co-emperor of Nicephorus.

The unity of the Roman Empire was thus saved, but Charlemagne, not at all impressed by the *Donatio Constantini*, regarded himself as master of Italy and Rome. Inspired by Augustine's writing on the City of God on earth which he misunderstood, and the theory that a Christian king, another Melchisedech, was not only king but also priest, he introduced another political theory in the West and ruled not only over the Western part of the former Roman Empire, but also over the Church and the pope.[8]

[7] Mansi, *Concilia*, 12, col. 985.
[8] A. Fliche and V. Martin, *op. cit.*, VI. For the political theories of

All this endangered the freedom of the Church and the old practice of the papal election by the Romans. Louis I confirmed to the Romans their right to elect the sovereign pontiff, but limited this freedom in 824, demanding that the pope should take an oath of loyalty to the emperor before his consecration. Lothar decreed that one could proceed to the consecration of a pope only after an order given by the emperor and in the presence of his envoys. Louis II provoked a short schism, favoring his own candidate against Benedict III, who had been chosen by the Romans. Benedict's successor Nicholas I was elected and ordained in the presence of Louis II.

The Romans disliked this intervention. Stephen V (885-891) was elected and consecrated without the knowledge of Charles the Fat, the last Carolingian emperor, and afterward the election of the popes was in the hands of Roman aristocracy. This kind of *modus vivendi* was acceptable to Constantinople, the more so as a great part of the aristocracy was rather pro-Byzantine.

However, this *modus vivendi* was ended by Otto I. Irritated by John XII and in difficulties with Roman parties, Otto I crossed the Alps, had himself crowned in Pavia as king of Italy, and was anointed in 962 in Rome by the pope as emperor. Otto wanted to become master even of the Italian provinces which were under Byzantine sovereignty. He sent Bishop Liutprand of Cremona to Constantinople with the request for a Byzantine bride for his son, expecting that Emperor Nicephorus Phocas would give away the Byzantine provinces as a dowry with the bride. The offer was received with the greatest displeasure, and the chapters in which Liutprand describes the reaction of the Byzantines to this outrage illustrate better than anything else how large the gap between East and West had grown.[9]

Otto I renewed the constitution of 824, replaced John XII by Leo VII and forced the Romans to promise not to ordain any pope before he had taken an oath of fidelity to the emperor

---

Charlemagne, cf. F. Dvornik, *The Making of Central and Eastern Europe* (London, 1949), pp. 39ff.

[9] *Monumenta Germaniae Historica* (Scriptores, 3), pp. 273-339, 347-63.

in the presence of his envoys. This meant abolition of free election. Two popes—Leo VIII and John XIII—were elevated to the papal throne by Otto.

This almost complete control of the Roman pontificate by the Franks displeased the Byzantines. In order to protect his Italian provinces—attacked in 968 by Otto—against the Franks and against the popes under Frankish obedience, Emperor Nicephorus Phocas forbade the use of the Latin rite in the provinces of Apulia and Calabria, and he created a new metropolitan See in Otranto with five bishoprics, which was put under the jurisdiction of Constantinople. It should be stressed that the tragic drama in 1054 had also a prelude in Apulia, provoked by similar reasons.

Pope John XII, in a letter in which he recommended Otto I to Nicephorus, called the latter "emperor of the Romans". This shows that the Westerners were forgetting the old idea of a single Roman Empire, recognizing a Roman Empire of the West with a Western emperor who should be crowned by the pope in Rome.

In spite of these dissensions, it seemed that the two Empires might again become united. Emperor John Tzimisces (969-976) consented to the marriage of his niece Theophano with Otto I's son in 972. Rome and Constantinople seemed again in good relations. However, the Byzantines did not renounce their right to influence the elections of popes. They favored the national party in Rome which had elected Boniface VII and offered him asylum when he had to cede his throne to Benedict VII, a candidate of Otto II. Theophano, the imperial widow (983), let the Romans elect their candidate, John XV (985-990), who was also supported by the pro-Byzantine party. Otto III (991-1002) chose his relative Gregory V as successor to John XV, but the pro-Byzantine party supported the Greek Philagathos from Calabria as John XVI. He was deposed by Otto III who appointed as Gregory's successor the learned Gerbert as Silvester II (999-1003).[10] In spite of all this, it is

[10] For details and bibliography, cf. V. Grumel, "Les préliminaires du schisme de Michel Cérulaire, ou la question romaine avant 1054," in *Revue des études byzantines* 10 (1953), pp. 1-23.

possible that, had Otto III lived longer, Constantinople and Rome would have been able to come to a new and durable understanding. He was a son of a Byzantine princess, knew Greek, introduced Byzantine ceremonial at his court, and his second request for a Byzantine bride, transmitted by Arnulf, Archbishop of Milan, was received in Constantinople very favorably; but before his bride could reach Rome, Otto III died.[11]

Under Otto's successor, Henry II (1002-1024), the rivalry between the imperial and the pro-Byzantine parties continued. John XVII and John XVIII were certainly accepted by Byzantium, and perhaps also Sergius IV. After his death (1012) Emperor Henry II confirmed the candidate of the pro-imperial party, Benedict VIII, who crowned Henry II in 1014 according to a new ceremonial, symbolically giving him suzerainty over the universal empire.

Under the reign of Benedict VIII events took place which brought a new actor on the Italian political field and which were to have a direct influence on the tragic events of 1054. Melo, a rich merchant of Bari, led an insurrection against the Greek governor of Apulia. When defeated, he took refuge in Capua. At the famous shrine of the Archangel Michael on the Mount of Gargano, Melo became acquainted with a group of Normans who had stopped there when returning from Jerusalem. Seeing that the Norman knights were interested in profitable adventure in Italy, he persuaded them to organize an expedition which he would lead to Apulia; there they could gain a rich booty after defeating the Greeks.[12]

A band of adventurous Normans arrived in Capua in 1015 or 1016. During their visit in Rome, the pope put the Normans in contact with Lombard princes who were also jealous of the Byzantines. Melo succeeded in recruiting some Lombard contingents and, with the Normans, invaded Apulia in 1017. However, Melo's army was defeated. Melo took refuge at Henry's

---

[11] For details, cf. F. Dvornik, *The Making of Central and Eastern Europe, op. cit.*, pp. 136ff.

[12] J. Gas, *L'Italie méridionale et l'empire byzantin* (Paris, 1904), pp. 399ff.

court in Bamberg, but the Norman adventurers stayed in Italy in the service of Lombard principalities waiting for another, more favorable occasion.

In spite of the growing estrangement between the Byzantine East and the Latin West in the 10th and 11th centuries, there is no reliable indication that Rome and Constantinople were already in open schism. The emperors of Constantinople continued to regard themselves as the only rulers appointed by God as leaders of Christianity. Rome was regarded as part of their empire. Naturally, they were interested in the person of the pope whose leading position in the Church was recognized by their legislation from Justinian I on. They were ready to accept the pope elected by the Romans, but they resented the growing influence of the Frankish kings—whose imperial title they did not recognize—in the elections of the bishops of Rome. This explains the frictions between Rome and Constantinople since the Franks had taken over the rule of Italy and Rome. Basically, however, the Byzantines recognized the primacy of Roman bishops in the Church.

With the Frankish rule over a great part of Italy and especially over Rome, some Frankish and Germanic features penetrated into the Roman Church which became more dangerous for the union between East and West than the political bickering between the two powers. One of the most important innovations— which could only increase the estrangement, since it touched upon the teaching of the Church—was the introduction of the *Filioque*[13] into the Nicene Creed. The Franks had taken over this custom from Spain where it had originated, but the popes, respecting the belief of the Greeks who regarded any addition to the Nicene Creed as unacceptable, resisted their request that

---

[13] *Filioque* means "and from the Son". It concerns here the formulation and the doctrine of the proceeding of the Holy Spirit from the Father *and from the Son* (*Filioque*). While the ancient Byzantine Church accepted the doctrine, although with detailed differences in the declaration, the formula *and from the Son* was not incorporated into the Creed. In the East the conception prevailed that after the Council of Ephesus (431) not a single change could be brought into the text of the Creed.

this addition should be declared as obligatory for the whole Church.

It apears that Pope Sergius (1009-1012) after his consecration was the first to send to the Byzantine patriarch with his enthronement letter, as was the custom, the Nicene Creed with the addition of *Filioque*. The Patriarch of Constantinople Sergius II (999-1019) rejected this. It is possible that the names of the popes ceased to be listed in the *dyptika*—lists of commemoration—in Constantinople from this time on. Nicetas of Nicaea who in the 11th century had composed a treatise on the Greek schism[14] speaks about a schism under the patriarchate of Sergius, but he confesses his ignorance of the reasons for this rupture. This indicates that if there were any, they had no durable consequences on the relations between East and West.

Another Germanic custom introduced into the Church administration profoundly transformed Western Christianity. Unable to conceive of the possibility of any property being vested in a society or organization as was recognized by Roman law, the Germanic nations regarded all ecclesiastical institutions founded by a layman as the property of the founders (*Eigenkirchen*—proprietary churches). Naturally, the founders claimed the right to invest anybody whom they chose with the property of their foundations. The consequence of this was the curtailment of the power of the bishops who could dispose freely only of churches and abbeys which they had founded.

This custom of proprietary churches, combined with the Germanic feudal system, strengthened the hands of the secular princes. It helped the Ottos to make of the Church a *Reichskirche*, absolutely devoted to the king, and curtailed the rights of the popes in Church administration.

This practice was bound to generate many abuses—appointment of laymen to richly endowed abbeys, simony, marriage of priests—abuses responsible for the decadence of the Western Church in the 10th and 11th centuries. This situation provoked

---

[14] *Patrologia Graeca (P.G.)*, 120, cols. 717ff.; cf. F. Dvornik, *Byzance et la Primauté Romaine, op. cit.*

reform movements. The Abbey of Cluny started the reform of monastic life. Unfortunately, the other reformist movement which attacked the abuses among the secular clergy did not start in Rome, but in Lorraine and Burgundy where the French and German kings did not possess enough power to stop a movement dangerous to their pretensions.

The reformers saw the root of the abuses in the theocratic system of priest-kings introduced by Charlemagne, and the only remedy in strengthening the power of the papacy not only over the Church, but also over the princes. In giving to the idea of the Roman primacy the largest definition, they extended the direct jurisdiction of Rome over all patriarchs and clergy in the East, having little comprehension of the exceptional position Byzantium occupied in the Christian world. They also ignored that there were no proprietary churches in the East, no feudal system hampering the activity of the bishops, no spread of simoniacal practice, and that the Eastern clergy was legally married, only the monks and bishops being bound to celibacy. Had the reform movement started in Italy, it is possible that such a generalization would not have developed.

Thus it happened that the reformers had contributed to the collapse of the last serious attempt to regularize the relations between Rome and Constantinople. In 1024 Emperor Basil II (976-1025) and Patriarch Eustathius addressed themselves to Pope John XIX with a proposal to end the frictions between Rome and Constantinople by a declaration that both Churches were ecumenical in their own spheres. At that time, Basil II was at the height of his power. He was making preparations to invade Sicily, then in the hands of the Arabs, and he was also anxious to strengthen his position in central Italy. An entente with the pope was desirable and he hoped that peaceful relations between Rome and Constantinople would be assured by the proposed declaration. This could also end the frictions between the Latins and Greeks in Italian Byzantine provinces.

If we can trust Raoul Glaber, whose chronicle is our main source for this episode, the Byzantines had in mind a declaration that would confirm the ordinances given to Rome and Constantinople by Justinian I, Phocas and Justinian II, because Glaber affirms that the Greeks were ready to recognize the supreme power of the first patriarch over the whole Church.

The news of these negotiations spread among the reformers; ignorant of the religious developments in the East and anxious to strengthen the power of the papacy, they claimed that the Greeks wanted to buy the primacy over the Church from the pope. The pope was attacked by many reformers and, intimidated by this emotion, refused the Greek offer.

After the death of John XIX the struggles for the possession of the pontifical chair continued. Henry III (1039-1056) convoked synods for the deposition of three popes and directly appointed three others. The third of his nominees was his own uncle, Leo IX (1049-1054), former bishop of Toul. The new pope was an ardent reformer, and in order to regularize his nomination, he asked to be elected by the Roman clergy and people. With him the reformative movement had reached Rome. The pope chose his most intimate councillors—the monks Humbert and Hildebrand and Archbishop Frederick of Lorraine—from among the most zealous reformers.

Leo IX started feverish activity for introduction of the reformers' principles in Italy, convoking synods, deposing simoniac bishops and defending ecclesiastical property against the pretensions of nobles. He was determined to strengthen his authority and to impose his reforms even in Latin communities under Byzantine political suzerainty. The most important synod was held in 1050 in Siponto. From the reports of the activities of his reformers we can conclude that some of the decrees voted at this synod were directed against certain Greek usages adopted in southern Italy and especially in Apulia. This was a dangerous move because Byzantium was jealously watching for any Frankish or papal activity in this part of its empire.

Leo's partner in Byzantium was Patriarch Michael Cerularius (1043-1058), perhaps the most ambitious and strong-willed prelate in Byzantine history. As a layman he instigated a conspiracy against Emperor Michael IV, hoping to replace him on the imperial throne. After the collapse of the revolt he was exiled, became a monk and turned his ambition to a supreme career in the Church. He became patriarch under the ineffective Emperor Constantine IX Monomachus; fully conscious of the dignity of his office and biased against the Latins, he was determined to strengthen his authority in Byzantine Italy.

There were some indications that his relations with Rome could have developed peacefully. Leo IX regularized his position by accepting the papal dignity only after having been elected by the Romans. This made him acceptable in Byzantium. Michael Cerularius seems to have been favorably impressed by the personage of Leo because visitors from Italy had informed him about the piety, noble sentiments and learning of the new pope.[15] However, he might have become suspicious when he learned that the pope had appointed Humbert "archbishop of all Sicily", probably in 1050.[16] Sicily was a Byzantine possession then occupied by the Arabs, and the Byzantines were making great efforts to recover the island. We know that Humbert's main argument for the extension of papal power was the *Donatio Constantini* which also included Sicily. This might have been the first stumbling block in the relations between the two prelates.

However, Michael seems to have been more alarmed by the activity of the reformers in Byzantine possessions in Italy. In order to defend his rights in Italy, which he thought menaced by the Latins, he started an offensive. As a countermeasure he ordered all Latin institutions in Constantinople to accept the Greek rite, closing monasteries and churches which had refused to comply. Such a measure was not warranted, even if we accept the possibility that some parishes in Apulia which were of the Greek rite had been persuaded to return to Roman obedience and liturgy.

At the same time Cerularius invited the Archbishop of Achrida to warn the Greek and Latin communities agains the offensive

---

[15] *P. G.*, 120, col. 784 for Michael's letters.
[16] A. Michel, *op. cit.*, I, p. 77.

movement. Leo of Achrida addressed a letter to the Latin bishop of Trani in Apulia, in which he attacked some Latin customs, especially the use of unleavened bread in the eucharist.[17]

The circulation of the latter in Byzantine possessions of Italy stirred up the sentiments of the inhabitants, and this was very unwelcome even to the emperor because a new danger had started to menace his Italian possessions. The Normans were again invading Apulia. Invited by another adventurer, Ardonine of Milan, who had been given command of some cities in Apulia by the Greeks, the Normans, whose numbers had grown, defeated the Byzantines and took possession of a great part of the province. Not content with this conquest they started to pillage and annex other cities, and they plundered the territory of the papal patrimony as well.

The pope was forced to take some protective action. He occupied Benevento and made preparations for a war against the Normans. Being unable to collect an army which could curb the Normans, he looked for an ally. The most logical one was the Emperor of Constantinople whose possessions were also in danger. Probably in order to strengthen the loyalty of the Latin population, the Emperor appointed as the commander-in-chief and governor of Apulia a Latin, Argyros (1051). Unfortunately, Argyros was especially disliked by Cerularius. Fearing that such an appointment might spell the end of Byzantine ecclesiastical sway in southern Italy, the patriarch strove to the utmost to prevent it, but without success. Argyros started negotiations with the pope and Leo IX welcomed the offer. However, their troops were routed in June, 1053, by the Normans who took the pope prisoner and placed him under a strong guard for a year in Benevento.

Seeing that anti-Latin sentiments had grown among the Greeks in Italy as a consequence of Leo of Achrida's letter, the pope asked Humbert to refute Achrida's accusations. The cardinal composed a very bitter and biased treatise; however, this was not published because, in the meantime, the emperor sent an embassy

---

[17] *P.G.,* 120, cols. 835-44.

to the pope; this embassy also brought a conciliatory missive to the pope from the patriarch. Leo IX decided to conclude an alliance and to send Humbert, Frederick of Lorraine and the Bishop of Amalfi as legates to the emperor. Humbert was charged to answer the patriarch's letter. However, Cerularius refused to receive the legates because the letter contained an attack against his title of ecumenical patriarch, a denial of the second place in the hierarchy to the patriarch of Constantinople and an expression of doubt about the legitimacy of Cerularius' elevation.

The cardinal, offended by the patriarch's behavior, published his treatise against Leo's letter in which he attacked violently many customs of the Greek Church; furthermore, in his disputation with the monk Stethatos, he accused the Greeks of suppressing the *Filioque* in the Creed. He probably thought that, in discrediting the patriarch to the clergy, he could, with the help of the emperor, overthrow him. Contrary to his expectations, the Greek clergy, offended by this attack, gathered in support of the patriarch. The emperor's attempt at restoration of good understanding remained unsuccessful and the embittered Humbert deposited the famous bull of excommunication of the patriarch on the altar of Hagia Sophia and left Constantinople.[18]

The contents of the bull profoundly shocked not only the patriarch but also the emperor. The latter allowed the patriarch to convoke a local synod which condemned the bull as full of unjust attacks against Greek customs and excommunicated the legates, calling them envoys not of the pope but of Argyros.[19]

Thus it happened that the papal action, meant to conclude an alliance and strengthen the union with Constantinople, ended with a new rupture more fateful than any other in the past. Cerularius was greatly responsible for it, and he was blamed by Peter, patriarch of Antioch, for his anti-Latin animosity. Humbert who misunderstood so tragically the mentality of the Byzan-

[18] *Patrologia Latina*, 143, cols. 930-74, 1001-4.
[19] *P.G.*, 120, cols. 736ff. The documents concerning the schism of 1054 were republished by C. Will, *Acta et Scripta quae de controversis ecclesiae graecae et latinae saeculo undecimo composita extant* (Leipzig/ Marburg, 1861) (reprint: Frankfurt a M., 1963).

tines carries an even heavier responsibility for his rash and offensive action.

Only the patriarch was excommunicated by Humbert, and the validity of this act is doubtful because Leo IX was already dead at that time. The synod excommunicated only the legates, abstaining from any attack on the pope or on the Latin Church. Thus, the schism between Rome and Constantinople was not yet concluded, and in the following period several popes and emperors reopened negotiations toward a union.[20] They could not succeed because the Byzantines, faithful to their political ideology, could not understand the development of the Latin political speculation which, under Gregory VII, had culminated in a new theocratic theory, proclaiming the superiority of spiritual power over the temporal. The Crusades, although originally intended to promote a union, at the end made the rift even deeper. The first open schismatic act happened in Antioch, reconquered by the Crusaders, when their leader Bohemond I appointed a Latin patriarch. The most fateful event was the conquest of Constantinople in 1204 by the Fourth Crusade, followed by the plundering of the city and its churches. The destruction of the Byzantine Empire by the Crusaders and the elevation of a Latin patriarch in Constantinople consummated the schism for centuries to come.

[20] For details cf. W. Norden, *Das Papsttum und Byzanz* (Berlin, 1903). Cf. also F. Dvornik, "Constantinople and Rome," in *Cambridge Mediaeval History,* 4 (1966).

The Sentences of Excommunication and Their Revocation (1054)

The Bull of Cardinal Humbert, July 16, 1054

Humbert[1] *by the grace of God Cardinal-bishop of the Holy Roman Church; Peter, Archbishop of the Amalfitans; Frederick, Deacon and Chancellor, to all the sons of the Catholic Church:*

The Holy Roman Apostolic See, first of all the Sees, to whom, as the head, the care of all the Churches most particularly belongs, has seen fit to send us as nuncios to this imperial city for the sake of the peace and good of the Church, to see if the rumors persistently reaching its ears from such an important city were in fact true. First, then, let the glorious emperor, the clergy and people of this city of Constantinople and the whole Catholic Church know that we have found here at once a deep sense of joy in the Lord and a grave cause of sadness. The pillars of empire and the wise and honorable citizens of this town are most Christian and orthodox. But as for Michael, called by the title of Patriarch,[2] and those who share his folly, they are in fact sowing

---

[1] The text is to be found in the *Brevis et Succinta commemoratio*, composed by Cardinal Humbert himself, in *P.L.* CXLLIII, col. 1001. The translation (French) here and also nn. 2-13 are taken from the article by M. Jugie, "Le schisme de Michel Cerularius," in *Echo d'Orient* (1937), pp. 460ff.

[2] What could be more tactless than to refuse the title of patriarch to the bishop of Constantinople, and to do so in the name of the old Roman triarchy, a theory more subtle than convincing, which by the 11th century had virtually no application?

an abundant crop of heresies each day in the bosom of this city. Like the Simoniacs, they sell the gift of God;[3] like the Valesians they make their guests[4] eunuchs in order to raise them not only to clerical orders but even to the episcopate;[5] like the Arians, they rebaptize those who have already been baptized in the name of the Blessed Trinity, and particularly the Latins;[6] like the Donatists, they affirm that outside the Greek Church the true Church of Christ and her true sacrifice and true baptism have disappeared from the entire world; like the Nicolaitans, they allow the ministers of the holy altar to contract marriage and demand this right for them;[7] like the Severians, they declare the law of Moses cursed;[8] like the Pneumatomachi, they have suppressed the progression of the Holy Spirit *a Filio* in the symbol;[9] like the Manicheans, they declare among other things that fermented bread is animated;[10] like the Nazarenes, they attach such importance to the fleshly purity of the Jews that they refuse to baptize infants before their eighth day, even if they are in danger of death; they likewise refuse communion or, if they are still pagan, baptism to women in childbirth or at the time of their periods,

[3] Was it proper to accuse the Byzantine church of simony at a time when the Latin Church was still trying to rid itself of the same curse?

[4] *Hospites suos castrant.* Cerularius' translators have rendered *hospites* as *pariokous.* For the Valesians, see St. Augustine, *De haeresibus,* in *Patr. Lat.* XLII, col. 132.

[5] The Orthodox later accused the Romans of guaranteeing pure voices for their choirs by the practice of castration. Humbert would certainly have been hard pressed to justify this strange accusation by solid proof, other than isolated cases.

[6] This can only refer to rare cases of abuse, and not to current practice. Throughout the whole of the Middle Ages, and for several centuries after the schism, the Orthodox received Latins into their Church, usually through a simple form of abjuration and profession of faith, and sometimes through anointing with chrism.

[7] These words imply that the Orthodox allowed ordained priests to marry. In fact the decrees of the council *in Trullo* forbade all marriage to subdeacons, deacons and priests after their ordination.

[8] An obviously exaggerated accusation, deduced from arguments against unleavened bread.

[9] Humbert is talking nonsense here.

[10] An illusion to the symbolic argument in favor of leavened bread. By a similar process, certain anti-Latin polemicists were to accuse the Latin Church of the heresy of Apollinarius because they used unleavened bread.

even if they are likewise in danger of death; furthermore, as they leave their beard and hair to grow, they refuse communion to those who, after the custom of the Roman Church, cut their hair and shave their beards. Michael, after having received the written admonitions of our master, Pope Leo, has refused to amend all these errors and many other culpable acts. Furthermore, he has refused audience and speech to us legates who wished to put an end to such grave abuses, and he has refused to allow us to say Mass in the churches. He had already ordered the closing of the churches of the Latins, treating them as Azymites and persecuting them in word and deed, going so far as to anathematize the Holy See in her children and daring to give himself the title of Ecumenical Patriarch against the wish of the same Holy See. And so, unable to bear these unheard-of injuries and outrages addressed to the first Apostolic See, and seeing the Catholic faith thereby gravely impaired in many ways, by the authority of the holy and indivisible Trinity of the Apostolic See whose ambassadors we are and of all the holy orthodox Fathers of the Seven Councils,[11] we sign against Michael and his followers the anathema which our Holy Pope has pronounced against them unless they amend their ways.

Let Michael the neophyte, who without right bears the title of Patriarch, whom a human fear alone has led to take the monastic habit, at present charged with the gravest accusations, and with him Leo who calls himself bishop of Achrida, and Michael's chancellor Constantine [the Greek translation has *Nicephoros*] who has sacrilegiously trodden underfoot the sacrifice of the Latins, and all those who follow them in the above-mentioned errors and presumptuous temerities—let all those come under the *anathema, Maranatha,*[12] with the Simoniacs, Valesians, Arians, Donatists, Nicolaitans, Severians, Pneumatomachi, Manicheans,

---

[11] It is strange that Humbert should only mention seven Councils, forgetting the eighth which condemned Photius. This must be simple forgetfulness and not a diplomatic precaution.

[12] Humbert really seems to be ignorant of the true meaning of this expression ("O Lord, come!") which he brandishes against his opponents like a scarecrow!

Nazarenes and all the heretics, and even more with the devil and his angels, unless they repent. Amen, amen, amen! [13]

Let anyone who persists in attacking the faith of the Holy Roman Church and its sacrifice be anathema, *Maranatha,* and not considered as a Catholic Christian, but as a *prozymite* heretic! Fiat, fiat, fiat! [14]

II

THE REPLY OF MICHAEL CERULARIUS
IN THE SYNODAL ACT OF JULY 24, 1054

On July 24,[15] a day by custom devoted to an exposition of the Fifth Council, this impious document[16] was once again pronounced anathema in the presence of a crowd, as were those who had published and written it, or, in one way or another, given their consent or encouragement to it.

For the everlasting dishonor and perpetual condemnation of those who have hurled such blasphemies against our God, the original text of this impious and execrable document, drawn up by wicked men, has not been burned [17] but placed in the sacristy archives.

Be it known, furthermore, that on the 20th day of this same month, the day when all those who blasphemed against the orthodox faith were declared anathema, all the metropolitans and

[13] The Greek translation which Michael Cerularius put in his *Synodal Edict* (cf. infra, N.d.l.R.) is a faithful one, differing from the original only in insignificant details. Michael had no need to omit anything from a document that played into his hands only too well. Cf. *P.G.* 120, cols. 741-46.

[14] This little piece, a shorter excommunication, was added by the legates in Constantinople and spoken aloud. The expression *prozymite* was invented by Humbert. It must mean "defender of leavened bread", thus throwing back the sobriquet *azymite* coined by Cerularius.

[15] This text forms the end of a synodal note drawn up by Cerularius during the session of July 24, 1054, in which he mentions the events that had just taken place in the capital.

[16] Humbert's bull, that is.

[17] In spite of the fact that the emperor of Constantinople had ordered the document to be burned.

bishops staying in the town were present, together with other dignitaries staying with us.[18]

III

THE JOINT DECLARATION OF DECEMBER 7, 1965 [19]

Filled with gratitude to God for the favor granted them, in his mercy, of meeting in brotherly charity in the holy places where the mystery of our salvation was consummated by the death and resurrection of the Lord Jesus, and the Church born of the outpouring of the Holy Spirit, Pope Paul VI and Patriarch Athenagoras I have not lost sight of the aim they set themselves at that time, that each would in the future lose no opportunity of making any gesture that, inspired by charity, could help the development of the brotherly relations so begun between the Roman Catholic Church and the Orthodox Church of Constantinople. They are sure that in this way they are responding to the call of divine grace which today is bringing the Roman Catholic and Orthodox Churches, and indeed all Christians, to overcome their differences so that they may again be "one" as the Lord Jesus asked his Father that they should be.

Among the obstacles on the road to development of these brotherly relations of trust and esteem is the memory of those distressing decisions, acts and incidents which led to the sentence of excommunication pronounced on Patriarch Michael Cerularius and two other persons in 1054 by the legates of the Roman See, led by Cardinal Humbert, who in their turn were the object of a similar sentence pronounced by the Patriarch and the Synod.

It is not possible to make the events of that particularly troubled period of history other than what they were. But today, now

[18] The permanent synod.
[19] The joint Declaration of Pope Paul VI and Patriarch Athenagoras I. It was read in French during the public session of the Council of Dec. 7, 1965, and at the same time at the Phanar of the Patriarchate of Constantinople. The French text was published by *L'Osservatore Romano* on Dec. 8, 1965. (At least one version already published in the English press suffers from serious defects of translation—*Trans.*)

that a more serene and equitable judgment has been pronounced on them, we must recognize the excesses with which they were tainted and which led eventually to consequences far exceeding, as far as we can judge, the intentions and provisions of their authors, whose censures concerned the persons they were aimed at and not the Churches themselves, and were not taken by them as breaking ecclesiastical communion between the Sees of Rome and Constantinople.

This is why Pope Paul VI and Patriarch Athenagoras I, in his Synod, sure of expressing the common desire for justice and the unanimous sentiment of charity of their faithful, and recalling the Lord's precept: "So if you are offering your gift at the altar, and there remember that your brother has something against you, leave your gift there before the altar and go; first be reconciled to your brother, and then come and offer your gift" (Mt. 5, 23-24), declare with one accord that they:

1. Regret the offensive words, unfounded reproaches and unworthy actions which, on both sides, marked or accompanied the unfortunate events of that period.

2. Regret equally and efface from the memory and presence of the Church the sentences of excommunication that followed them, the memory of which acts to our own day are an obstacle to our drawing together in charity, and consign them to oblivion.

3. Deplore, lastly, the unfortunate precedents and later developments which, influenced by various factors such as misunderstanding and mutual distrust, led in the end to the actual breaking-off of ecclesiastical communion.

Paul VI and Athenagoras I, with his Synod, both realize that this gesture of justice and mutual pardon cannot in itself put an end to the differences, both old and new, that exist between the Roman Catholic and the Orthodox Churches. These will be overcome through the purifying of men's hearts by the Holy Spirit, setting aside historical wrongs and bringing an effective will to a common understanding and expression of the faith of the apostles and its requirements.

They hope, nevertheless, that this gesture they are making will be acceptable to God, ever ready to forgive us as we forgive each other, and appreciated by the whole Christian community, but particularly by the Roman Catholic and Orthodox Churches, as the expression of a sincere mutual desire for reconciliation and an initiation to further dialogue in a spirit of mutual confidence, goodwill and charity, the dialogue which will, under God's help, bring them to live once again, to the benefit of souls and the furtherance of the kingdom of God, in the full communion of faith, brotherly harmony and sacramental life which they shared for the first thousand years of the life of the Church.

Arno Burg, A.A. / *Nijmegen, Netherlands*

Postscript

In July, 1054, the papal legates, Cardinal Humbert, Archbishop Petrus and Deacon Fridericus, pronounced excommunication on the Patriarch of Constantinople, Michael Cerularius. The Patriarch replied with a similar excommunication of the Roman envoys.

About nine centuries later, on December 7, 1965, at the close of Vatican Council II, both Churches, simultaneously in Rome and Constantinople, expressed their regret at this excommunication and resolved to erase it "from the memory and the life of the Church".

What is the meaning and import of this joint act?

F. Dvornik has pointed out in his article that the disintegration of East and West caused these two worlds to move farther and farther apart. Political, social and psychological factors, the difference in mentality and environment and the lack of communication between East and West contributed to the growth of this frequently undesired estrangement into rivalry and eventually into envy and hatred. Liturgical, disciplinary and theological characteristics were consequently seen as deviations from the one sanctifying doctrine and discipline—as shortcomings, errors and heresies. In this way, the division between East and West slowly grew wider.

Fewer and fewer spectacular clashes occurred as contacts between the two worlds became less and less frequent, but those that did take place left scars. It was not until the 13th century that the schism finally came about.

The capricious fortunes of later history resulted in the importance and significance of certain facts being greatly exaggerated
and being given too central a position, so that they attracted too
much attention. This was the case with the events of 1054. The
legal validity of the excommunication is certainly open to doubt[1]
and it is of course true that it affected only papal legates and a
Byzantine patriarch, and not their Churches. But, despite this,
it is impossible to deny the deep psychological significance that
the excommunication of 1054 rightly or wrongly acquired. "Ex-
aggerations, false accusations and the objectionable action in
which both sides incurred guilt in fact left such an unfavorable
impression behind that these excommunications have been interpreted by later generations as a decisive factor in the whole process of schism. All the bitterness and resentment between East
and West, have, so to speak, become crystallized in these con-
demnations." [2] Even until the very recent past, Cardinal Humbert's action of 1054 has to a great extent determined the unfavorable attitude of the Orthodox world toward Rome. The
lifting of the excommunication by both Constantinople and Rome
is a sign of their mutual desire to break down this psychological
barrier. Both sides regret the past, both have admitted that they
were in the wrong and both are ready to forget and forgive this
somber episode.

However, this does not mean that the division between Rome
and the Orthodox world has ceased to exist. Only the numerically
small group of Constantinople was directly involved in this, and
the principle of autocephaly[3] means that each Church is independent. It was clearly agreed at the Third Panorthodox Conference of Rhodes (1964) of the Orthodox Churches that each
Church is free, on its own authority, to have fraternal relationships with Rome, but is not thereby empowered to speak in the
name of the whole Orthodox world. Although the Patriarch of

[1] A. Michel, "Die Rechtsgültigkeit des römischen Bannes gegen Michael
Kerularios," in *Byzantinische Zeitschrift*, 42 (1943-9), pp. 193-205.

[2] C.-J. Dumont, "Un nouveau pas sur la voie de la réconciliation," in
Vers l'unité chrétienne, 18 (1965), p. 90.

[3] *Autos—kephalos:* each Church is "itself head".

Constantinople enjoys greater prestige than any other Church leader and is invested with a kind of honorary primacy in the Orthodox Churches, the immediate import of the lifting of the excommunication does not extend beyond the patriarchate of Constantinople. The action may be a hint to other Church leaders, and several of them will presumably take similar steps in the near future.

However, it is not surprising that Nikodim, the Metropolitan of Leningrad and one of the closest collaborators of Patriarch Alexei of Moscow, stated in an interview with the correspondent of the Russian agency, Tass, that the lifting of the excommunication by Constantinople was only a gesture on the part of a local Church and not an act of the whole Orthodox world. "The reunion of the Eastern and Western Churches can only be realized after serious theological consultation and joint cooperation." [4] He added that, from the Eastern point of view, a document like the *Decree on the Catholic Churches of the Eastern Rite* (issued during the Council) did not further ecumenical contacts. However, he used much milder language to Metropolitan Meliton of Heliopolis and Theira who visited the patriarchate of Moscow in March, 1966, on behalf of Athenagoras, the patriarch of Constantinople. He said that he regarded the lifting of the excommunication as "an act of brotherly love and a very favorable augury" and declared: "If this gesture can create a favorable climate between the two Churches, we welcome it with joy." [5]

It is obvious that centuries of estrangement, culminating in schism and resulting in continued hostility, cannot be cancelled out by one action. A new mental attitude is required, and this must be given time to develop. Nonetheless, a serious obstacle was removed and the way was cleared for further dialogue on December 7, 1965. This approach has made us all the more aware of the division, and this awareness is a very important condition if we are to be able to heal this division.

[4] *Soepi*, 33 (1966), n. 3, p. 10.
[5] *Soepi*, 33 (1966), n. 8, p. 3.

BIOGRAPHICAL NOTES

VICTOR CONZEMIUS: Born in Echternach, Luxembourg, he was ordained in 1955. He studied at the University of Fribourg in Switzerland, and at the Sorbonne and the Institut Catholique in Paris. He earned his degree in history in 1954, and was assigned to parish work for two years after ordination. Since 1958 he has devoted his time to scientific research in the historical field. At present he is engaged in research in Dublin, where he also teaches modern history. His published works, both books and articles, deal with historical subjects.

GIUSEPPE D'ERCOLE: Born April 16, 1906, in Guarcino, Italy, he was ordained in 1929 for the Diocese of Rome. After earning degrees in philosophy and theology, he became a Doctor of Canon Law. At present he is professor of the history of Canon Law at the Institutum Utriusque Iuris in Rome. He has numerous published works in Italian to his credit, dealing with many aspects of the law. He contributes to such reviews as *Apollinaris* and *Studia et Documenta Historiae et Iuris,* and is director of *Communio.* In preparation now are studies on the law and discipline in the Old and New Testaments and in the primitive Church.

MARIO ROSA: Born May 8, 1932, in Naples, he earned his degree in letters in 1955. Since then he has published many articles in Italian reviews on historical figures and on cultural and religious life in Italy since the Middle Ages. He collaborated in the preparation of an ecclesiastical history, and at present is preparing a study on the spread of the encyclopedia in Italy.

JOHANNES VAN LAARHOVEN: Born August 3, 1926, in Zevenbergen, the Netherlands, he pursued his theological studies after ordination at the Gregorian University in Rome. After an assignment as parish priest in the Netherlands, he became professor of church history at the major seminary, rector of the minor seminary, and is at present professor of church history at the Catholic University of Nijmegen. He has published a number of studies in various reviews dealing with church history, problems and reform.

JEAN LECLERCQ, O.S.B.: Born January 31, 1911, in Avesnes, France, he became a Benedictine and was ordained in 1936. He pursued his studies in his chosen field of historical science at various institutes of higher learning: the College of St. Anselm in Rome, the Institut Catholique in Paris, l'Ecole des Hautes Etudes, the College de France and l'Ecole des Chartes. He earned his doctorate in theology in 1943 in Paris, and he has honorary doctorates from the universities of Milan and Louvain. At present he is professor at the College of St. Anselm in Rome. Among his published works is one in Italian on the works of St. Bernard and one in French on the sources of Western spirituality. He contributes to such reviews as *Irénikon, Revue bénédictine, Etudes* and *Christus.*

HILARION PETZOLD: Born March 25, 1944, in Kirchen-Sieg, Germany, he is a member of the Orthodox Church in France. He pursued his studies at the Séminaire des Trois Saints Hiérarques of the Patriarchal Russian Exarchate in western Europe, and at the French Orthodox Institute of St. Denis in Paris. He has published a number of articles in German reviews on iconography and on imagery and symbolism in the Bible.

ROGER AUBERT: Born January 16, 1914, in Ixelles-Bruxelles, Belgium. After ordination, he earned his doctorate in philosophy in 1933, and his doctorate in theology in 1942. He was professor in the major seminary at Malines from 1944 to 1952 when he was appointed to the University of Louvain as professor of church history. He is director of the *Revue d'Histoire Eccl.* and of the *French Dictionary of Church History and Geography,* vice-president of the Belgian Commission on Church History, co-director of the new *Histoire de l'Eglise,* and member of many international historical societies. His many published works take up the subjects of Christian unity, 20th-century theology, the Vatican Council and Church history in general. He contributes to numerous reviews, among them the *Catholic Historical Review, Revista di Storia delle Chiesa in Italia, Revue d'Histoire Eccl.,* and *Lexikon für Theologie und Kirche.*

BORIS ULIANICH: Born February 12, 1925, in Pola (Istria), Italy, he pursued his studies in Rome. At present he is professor of church history and of modern history at the University of Bologna and a member of the "Centro di Documentazione" in that city. He has many published works in Italian in the historical field, and contributes regularly to such reviews as *Riv. di Storia della Chiesa in Italia, Rev. Storica Italiana, Studi Storici O.S.M.* and *Bibl. d'Humanisme et Rénaissance.* In preparation are two historical works, one on the Council of Trent and one on the attempts at unity from the end of the Council of Trent to the Thirty Years War.

HEIKO OBERMAN: Born October 15, 1930, in Utrecht, the Netherlands, he was ordained in 1958 in the Presbyterian Church, after having studied at the University of Utrecht, the Sekolah Tinggi in Indonesia and at Oxford University. He earned his doctorate in theology *cum laude* at Utrecht in 1957. He has taught at Harvard Divinity School, is a member of various Academies of Arts and Sciences, and at present is at the University of Tübingen. His published works, alone and in collaboration, include *Christianity Divided* (1961), *The Harvest of Medieval Theology* (1963), and *Forerunner of the Reformation* (1966). He is a contributor to *The Harvard Theological Review, Church History, Journal of Ecumenical Studies, Kerygma und Dogma* and others.

JAMES HENNESEY, S.J.: Born October 6, 1926, in Jersey City, he was ordained in 1957. He studied at Fordham University, Loyola University of Chicago, Woodstock College and the Catholic University of America. He earned an M.A. in history in 1960 and his doctorate in philosophy in 1963, both at Catholic University. He is associate professor of American church history at Gregorian University and lecturer in church history. His published works concentrate on Vatican Council I, particularly with American participation in the Council. His book *The First Council of the Vatican: the American Experience* (1963) is an example. He is a frequent contributor to such reviews as *America, Catholic Historical Review, Continuum, Theological Studies, Dialog and Catholic Mind,* and he is the author of several articles in the *Catholic Encyclopedia for School and Home* (1965).

CHARLES MOELLER: Born January 18, 1912, in Brussels, he was ordained in 1937. He pursued his studies at the University of Louvain, where he became a professor. The Holy Father recently appointed him Undersecretary of the Doctrinal Congregation (ex-Holy Office). He played a large role in the drawing up of the *Constitution on the Church* and the *Church in the Modern World,* two documents of Vatican Council II. Among his published works are the four volumes that have already appeared of *Littérature du XXe siècle et Christianisme,* some in collaboration. He is one of the founders of the Ecumenical Institute of Theological Research in Jerusalem, and a frequent contributor to reviews, including *Irénikon, Revue Nouvelle, Criterio* and *Revue d'Histoire Eccl.*

FRANCIS DVORNIK: Born August 14, 1893, in Chomyz, Czechoslovakia, he was ordained in 1916 for the Diocese of Olomouc. He earned a degree from the Ecole des Sciences Politiques in Paris in 1923 and a doctorate in letters from the Sorbonne in 1926. From 1928 to 1949 he taught church history in Prague. In 1941 he was named Berkbeck Lecturer at Trinity College of Cambridge University, and since 1949 he has been professor of Byzantine history at Harvard University. His many published works are devoted to the history of the Eastern Church. Among them are *The Schism of Photios, History and Legend* (1948), *The Making of Central and Eastern Europe* (1949), *The Idea of Apostolicity in Byzantium and the Legend of the Apostle Andrew* (1958), and *The Slavs in European History and Civilization* (1962). He is collaborating in the review *Dumbarton Oaks Papers* and is preparing studies due to appear in 1966 on early Christian and Byzantine political philosophy and on Byzantine Slavic missions scheduled for 1967.

ARNO BURG, A.A.: Born May 8, 1922, in 's-Hertogenbosch, the Netherlands, he became an Assumptionist and was ordained in 1949. He studied at the Pontifical Institute for Eastern Studies in Rome, where he earned his degree in Eastern sciences. From 1952 to 1958 he was professor of church history at the major Syrian seminary of Charfé, Lebanon. At present he is Secretary of Publications of *Het Christelijk Oosten* and Secretary of the Byzantine and ecumenical institute of Nijmegen. He is a contributor to the Dutch reviews *Het Christelijk Oosten* and *Katholiek Archief*, and he writes articles for the dictionary *Winkler Prins*.

International Publishers of CONCILIUM

ENGLISH EDITION
Paulist Press
Glen Rock, N. J., U.S.A.

Burns & Oates Ltd.
25 Ashley Place
London, S.W.1

DUTCH EDITION
Uitgeverij Paul Brand, N. V.
Hilversum, Netherlands

FRENCH EDITION
Maison Mame
Tours/Paris, France

GERMAN EDITION
Verlagsanstalt Benziger & Co., A.G.
Einsiedeln, Switzerland

Matthias Grunewald-Verlag
Mainz, W. Germany

SPANISH EDITION
Ediciones Guadarrama
Madrid, Spain

PORTUGUESE EDITION
Livraria Morais Editora, Ltda.
Lisbon, Portugal

ITALIAN EDITION
Editrice Queriniana
Brescia, Italy